TWO-MINUTE TIME OUTS

Daily Bible Meditations

JULIE BAKER

WESTBOW
PRESS®
A DIVISION OF THOMAS NELSON
& ZONDERVAN

WestBow Press books may be ordered through booksellers or by contacting:

WestBow Press
A Division of Thomas Nelson & Zondervan
1663 Liberty Drive
Bloomington, IN 47403
www.westbowpress.com
1 (866) 928-1240

ISBN: 978-1-9736-7159-6 (sc)
ISBN: 978-1-9736-7158-9 (hc)
ISBN: 978-1-9736-7160-2 (e)

Library of Congress Control Number: 2019911241

Print information available on the last page.

WestBow Press rev. date: 08/15/2019

Contents

Introduction

TWO-MINUTE TIME OUTS WITH JULIE BAKER

Each day has 86,400 seconds in it. Can you give God at least 120 of them? That's just two minutes!

My hope is that you will and that in just those few seconds, you will find encouragement to start your day, end it, or soak in over a second cup of coffee.

This body of work is just a portion of daily devotions I wrote for a radio program I had for years called TimeOut for Women. I've chosen and edited them so that they are appealing to both men and women. May they speak to you as God intends and encourage you in your daily spiritual journey!

Julie Baker

Day 1

JESUS IS THE LORD OF NEW BEGINNINGS

Several years ago, I was trying to fold a mountain—of clothes that is. Our entire king-sized bed was stacked sky high with a whole week's worth of family folding.

When the phone rang, I was relieved for a break in the routine. I was surprised when the voice on the other end was that of a Mom in one of my car pools. She was a woman that, frankly, I envied. Her husband held a prominent job as a respected professional, they lived in a huge, beautifully decorated home, and she drove a cute little red foreign sports car. AND she was gorgeous! She had it all—by outward appearances.

She sounded very weak and I soon discovered that she was calling me from the hospital. Slowly, she unfolded her story. She began: "Actually, I'm in the hospital because I tried to take my own life Tuesday evening. I've really made a mess of things, Julie. When I was a child I was physically abused and it led to drugs and alcohol. Even with all the wonderful things in my life, I really messed things up by having an affair. I thought he would marry me, but after I told my husband I was leaving him, I discovered that my lover was having an affair, cheating on me. Now I have no one and nothing to live for. Even God won't forgive me."

I was speechless. How do you respond to that? I silently prayed and asked the Lord to give me a verse, or any words of encouragement for her. At that moment, the Lord placed within my mind this message for her: "Tell her that I am the Lord of New Beginnings!" No matter what the circumstances of the past, Jesus can wipe the slate of the past clean and give us a new beginning.

A New Beginning for Onesimus

Philemon 1:17: "...welcome him as you would welcome me."

In the brief letter from Paul to Philemon, we learn that Philemon's slave, Onesimus, stole from Philemon then ran away—a deed punishable by death under Roman law of that day. Somehow, Onesimus catches up with Paul and Paul leads him to the Lord. Now Onesimus is a new person, forgiven and blameless. Second Corinthians 5:17 reminds us that "Therefore, if anyone is in Christ, he is a new creation; the old has gone, the new has come!"

With God, this new beginning was just that for Onesimus. In the spirit realm, God remembers his sin no more. However, in the natural, Onesimus still has to deal with the consequences of his previous actions.

Paul, therefore, demonstrates to us the beautiful example of what it means to be an intercessor. Like Jesus did for us, he placed himself between the master and slave and paved the way for reconciliation. Paul used beautiful expressions like: "I appeal to you for *my son,* Onesimus, who became my son while I was in chains" Philemon 1:10). "I am sending him—who is my very heart—back to you" (Philemon 1:12). "Welcome him as you would welcome me. If he has done you any wrong or owes you anything, charge it to me" (Philemon 1:17).

In many ways, Paul was offering to be a co-signer of a note bearing the life sentence of Onesimus. Paul's desire was that Philemon accept the fact that Onesimus was a new creation and that he deserved a new beginning.

The Word does not reveal to us whether Philemon accepted Onesimus back into his household or not, but we can assume that he did. The reunion must have been the dawning of a tear-filled new beginning.....

Day 3

A New Beginning for a Prostitute

I want to draw our attention to Rahab, who as you may recall, assisted Joshua and the Children of Israel in the capturing of Jericho. Although Josephus and other early scholars actually refer to her as an innkeeper, the Bible, describes Rahab as a prostitute.

As the story unfolds, Joshua sends two spies into Jericho to kinda scope things out to see if the city can be taken. It would seem that the two men ended up at Rahab's place seeking a place to stay. I wonder if Rahab already knew the true God from hearing about the Israelites, or whether the spies were actually the ones instrumental in sharing God's truth with her and converting her.

In any case, Rahab hides the spies and misdirects the authorities so that they make it safely back to their camp. In return, the spies guarantee the safety of Rahab and her family as long as she designates her place on the city wall by a scarlet rope hung from her window. The scarlet rope is reminiscent of the lamb's blood that the Children of Israel painted on their door posts during the Passover.

What is so awesome about this story is that even though Rahab had been labeled a prostitute, her conversion and confession of faith in the God of the Israelites gained her special recognition and a new beginning.

She is mentioned with honor in Hebrews 11:31, James 2:25, and when we read the genealogy of Christ in Matthew 1:5, guess whose name appears? Yes! Rahab—the prostitute—is listed as the mother of Boaz. Boaz married Ruth, and they begot Obed and on throughout the generations until we arrive at the birth of Christ. When we come to Christ, we no longer have a sinful past.

Day 4

RUTH THE MOABITE

Ruth was a Moabite. Moabites were detested in that day because they were a nation whose roots began through the incest of Lot and his two daughters. Ruth's mother-in-law, Naomi, was Hebrew, so when both women found themselves widowed, Naomi's heart took her back to her people.

Ruth wanted to go with her. One of the most beautiful statements ever made in the Bible was from Ruth to Naomi: "Where you go, I will go, and where you stay, I will stay. Your people will be my people and your God my God" (Ruth 1:16). Wow! What a credit to Naomi's character and life's example that her daughter-in-law would leave her own country to live in a foreign place with a foreign tongue worshiping the Hebrew God!

This was the turning point of a new beginning for Ruth. When she proclaimed that "Your God will be my God," she had no idea just how God would bless her commitment.

In that culture, a single woman was to come under the authority of the closest male kin, who was called her "Kinsman Redeemer." This person was Boaz. Boaz was the son of Salmon AND Rahab the prostitute! Eventually, Boaz and Ruth marry. Look at that family lineage! Boaz' mother was a prostitute and he married into THE most despicable ethnic group of that day! Yet, because they served the Lord of New Beginnings, their lineage was of little consequence. Both Rahab and Ruth are listed in the genealogy of Christ in Matthew 1. You see, when we come to Jesus, we are given new birth into a new family...a new beginning!

Day 5
FROM OLD TO NEW

Philippians 2:13 reminds us that "...it is God who works in you to will and to act according to his good purpose."

We have an acquaintance who just came to a saving knowledge of Jesus Christ and has experienced being reborn! While being very excited about this, we've also experienced some eye-brow-raising reactions. You see, we still see much of the "old" in this person, even though through salvation he is a "new creation!" This not only has confused us, but distressed us. Or it did until we came across this verse in Philippians.

I wanted to see *immediate* changes in this person's outward expressions and attitudes. In fact, I wanted to change this person myself and thought given enough time, certainly my insights and wisdom would make a huge difference! Philippians 2:13, however, reminds me that it is God...and Him alone, who works in a person and is able to change someone...not only on the inside, but on the outside.

In a way, I'm glad that this person isn't doing what many do when they come to Jesus: they get all cleaned up on the outside, giving the world the impression that they've got it all together, but are still filthy on the inside. This is hypocritical and God hates a hypocrite!

No, it's better for us to prayerfully stand beside a new Christian and pour love into them that will affect them on the inside. You see, people change from the inside out. And because working out their salvation is a process that takes time, we need to give them space to grow and evolve in their new-found relationship in Jesus Christ.

A new beginning is just that...new! Any change from the old way to the new way requires time and patience in our process of growth!

Day 6

THE DAMASCUS ROAD EXPERIENCE

Saul was a Jewish zealot who took great offence that anyone should proclaim a religion or worship experience contrary to what he considered to be THE correct one! He was busy persecuting the early Christians and intended to travel to Jerusalem to really let them have it. He had even secured a document from the High Priest that would allow these crazy people, claiming that Jesus was the Messiah, to be tried and punished for their beliefs.

As the story goes, Saul gets as far as the road to Damascus before he is literally struck blind in his steps. A light so much brighter than the sun engulfs him and a voice comes from the light saying: "Saul, Saul, why do you persecute me?" (Acts 9:4). Isn't this an interesting question? Saul thought he was persecuting irritating Christians; in reality, though, he was persecuting the Lord God of Heaven. All sin, regardless of its character, is ultimately directed against the Lord God.

Now, talk about changed! Talk about a new beginning! A devout Jew who did not believe in Christianity and certainly did not aspire to associate with Gentiles immediately began work as a missionary to the Gentiles. Why? Because the one who had been blind could now see.

On the way to Damascus, Saul met Jesus, and ironically, he who had been blind to the Gospel was now blind to the world. After he received the Holy Spirit, "something like scales fell off of his eyes and he could see again" (9:18). Now he could see Jesus.

Jesus may not reveal himself to us in a Damascus Road experience, but when we are given a new beginning, nothing in our past can separate us from the love of God!

Day 7

A New Beginning Thrown Away

Genesis 19 recounts the destruction of Sodom and Gomorrah. Because of Abraham's plea to the Lord, God was willing to spare the lives of Abraham's nephew, Lot, his wife and their two daughters who lived there.

One gets the impression that even though the city was so evil that God wanted to annihilate it, Lot and his family stuck to it like glue! One senses that they got so caught up in the glamor of the city life and all of the amenities, that they did not want to leave. Even if it meant their lives!

In the final moments when they could actually still get out of the city alive, they were not taking any steps, literally, to leave the city.

In fact, verse 16 says, "When Lot hesitated, the men (who were angels) grasped his hand and the hands of his wife and of his two daughters and led them safely out of the city, for the Lord was merciful to them." It sounds as if they had to be dragged, kicking and screaming from this place! It's still hard to comprehend why they would be willing to stay in a place that God promised to destroy.

God in his mercy was willing to afford them a new beginning, yet they were resisting it. They wanted to experience the old when God wanted to give them something new and obviously better. And you know the rest of the story. Although they had been commanded not to look back (and I'm guessing for their own safety so ghastly was the destruction with sulfur raining down from heaven), Lot's wife did and....the Bible says that she turned into a pillar of salt (Genesis 19:26).

Lot and his daughters end up living a pathetic existence in a cave.

What a tragic ending they didn't have to endure. They squandered their new beginning.

Are there times when we are forced out of a job, or a toxic relationship, only longing to stay? It's familiar and we feel that we are somehow giving something up that God won't repair or replace. That is not how God works. When we leave the old behind, He ALWAYS (in time) offers us something better...a new beginning.

Day 8

A NEW BEGINNING FORFEITED

Yesterday we looked at the lives of Lot and his family who squandered a new beginning. Today we want to look at the life of King Saul and how through disobedience he forfeited God's blessing after he had been offered a new beginning.

In First Samuel 10, Saul is anointed King of Israel through the prophet Samuel. Of Saul, Chapter 9:2 describes him as being "an impressive young man without equal among the Israelites—a head taller than any of the others." First Samuel 10:9 tells us that "...God changed Saul's heart and all these signs were fulfilled that day....The Spirit of God came upon him in power."

Wow! Saul had it all! God's anointing, natural ability, admiration of the nation, and most importantly, God's power through His spirit. Things just have to work out perfectly now, don't they?

Perhaps they could have, because God seemed to hand a new beginning on a silver platter for Saul. However, as we read through the rest of First Samuel, we find that disobeying God, allowing pride and jealousy to drive him mad, and losing touch with the power that positioned him as King leads him down a path of self-destruction.

To me one of the saddest verses in the Bible is in First Samuel 16:14 where the Word tells us that "the Spirit of the Lord had departed from Saul and an evil spirit...tormented him..."

Saul was given many opportunities to repent and be given yet another new beginning, but he chose not to. How it must grieve the heart of God when we reject his mercies, which are new every morning!

Day 9

A SINFUL WOMAN NO MORE!

John 8:1-11 relays the story of a woman caught in adultery. Sadly, the Jewish church leaders were trying to set a trap for Jesus. Since the Romans did not allow the Jews to carry out death sentences, Jesus would have been in conflict with the Roman law. However, if he said not to stone her, he would have been in conflict of supporting Jewish law. Doomed either way!

As they questioned Jesus, he bent down and wrote something in the sand. It's only speculation as to why he did this, however, when Jesus taught in the temple courts, it was customary for the teacher to sit and the students to stand. Perhaps it signified an important lesson was about to begin!

This woman must have been humiliated. She was guilty of sin (and, ahem, where was the man?) and it had been exposed in a very public, embarrassing way. However, she is not the only one. Jesus "straightened up." Did he then stand? Then says, "If any one of you is without sin, let him be the first to throw a stone at her" (John 8:7). Her accusers become achingly aware of their own sin.

One by one, the accusers slip away leaving only Jesus and the woman. You get the feeling that only then does Jesus look around and then at the woman. "Woman, where are they? Has no one condemned you?" "No one, sir." "Then neither do I condemn you" (John 8:11). Romans 8:1 encourages us that "Therefore, there is now no condemnation for those who are in Jesus Christ...."

While Satan accused her, Jesus affirmed her. People need encouragement to start over again. In verse 11 Jesus said, "Go now and leave your life of sin." First he forgave her, then he asked her to change and turn from her life of sin. Sometimes we get it backwards; we ask people to first change, THEN we will forgive them!

Jesus says, "Go," give it another try. No condemnation. I have given you a new beginning!

Day 10
THE NEW JERUSALEM

In Revelation 21:1 John writes: "Then I saw a new heaven and a new earth...He who was seated on the throne said, 'I am making all things new!'"

You and I are going to experience the most incredible new beginning when these prophesies are fulfilled. John tells us (verse 2) that "the first heaven and the first earth had passed away and...I saw the Holy City, the NEW Jerusalem, coming down out of heaven from God."

Second Peter 3:10 confirms this as Peter describes it thus: "But the day of the Lord will come like a thief. The heavens will disappear with a roar; the elements will be destroyed by fire, and the earth and everything in it will be laid bare. Since everything will be destroyed in this way, what kind of people ought you to be? You ought to live holy and godly lives as you look forward to the day of God and speed its coming. That day will bring about destruction of the heavens by fire, and the elements will melt in the heat. But in keeping with the promise we are looking forward to a NEW heaven and a NEW earth, the home of righteousness."

How do we obtain passage to this new and exciting place? We must experience a new beginning. A new birth. For those who have never received Jesus as their personal Savior, they must confess their sins and accept Christ as their Lord. To those of us who know the Lord, we must be careful to keep our newness fresh and untainted. This means confession WITH repentance; this means asking for a new portion of the Holy Spirit each day so that each day is a new beginning.

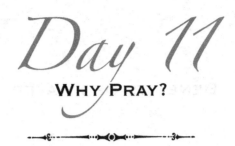

Day 11

WHY PRAY?

Have you ever asked yourself the question, "Why pray?" For most of us, I would guess that our response has to do with, "Hey, I will as long as there is something in it for me!"

And if you're like me, you've often looked at the Bible as an owner's operating manual on prayer. So, if we pray like this, we get this. If we say it this way and this often, this is what we get. I've often analyzed the Lord's Prayer and the Psalms trying to figure out the "secret" of getting prayers answered.

In Luke 11, Jesus teaches about prayer through a parable of a man's unbelievable rudeness. We have to remember that in that day the greatest embarrassment was to be an unprepared host. Because of his lack of preparation, the host bothers his neighbor in the middle of the night asking for bread to serve his guests. Jesus correlates this to the way we can approach God in prayer.

He says, "Ask and it will be given you; seek and you will find; knock and the door will be opened to you" (Luke 11:9). At first blush, it appears that Jesus is saying that we just have to ask enough times and boldly enough and anything we want we will get from God!

We must remember that through telling stories, Jesus often paints a picture for us, symbolizing and teaching a spiritual truth. Here he is doing more than giving us an instruction manual for prayer. No! He is giving us a picture of a RELATIONSHIP. He is trying to show us that God's priority is in the quality and closeness of our relationship. What Jesus is telling us is that God LOVES it when we boldly march into his throne room with any request at any time for any reason.

Day 12

BENEFITS OF PRAYER

Incredible benefits are available to us through the avenue of prayer! I John 1:9 reveals to us that prayer is the avenue through which we are granted forgiveness of sins: "If we confess our sins, he is faithful and just and will forgive us our sins and purify us from all unrighteousness."

Revelation 3:20 reminds us that Jesus never forces his way into our lives, but stands patiently knocking at our heart's door. When we open it to him, he fellowships with us. Prayer is the avenue through which we open that door: "Here I am! I stand at the door and knock. If anyone hears my voice and opens the door, I will come in and eat with him, and he with me."

Acts 1:24 reveals to us that prayer gives us discernment in decision-making: "Then they prayed, 'Lord, you know everyone's heart. Show us which of these two you have chosen to take over this apostolic ministry...'" God revealed that it was Mathias he had chosen.

Through prayer, we can receive peace and overcome fear. In John 14:27 Jesus says, "Peace I leave with you; my peace I give to you. I do not give to you as the world gives. Do not let your hearts be troubled and do not be afraid."

Ephesians 2:14 echoes this truth when Paul reminds us that "...he himself is our peace..."

I Peter 5:7 reminds us that through prayer we can be relieved of stress: "Cast all your anxiety on him for he cares for you." Jesus doesn't want to bear just part of our anxiety, he wants it all!

Finally, in John 16:24 Jesus says, "...Ask and you will receive, and your joy will be complete."

What incredible benefits we realize when we come to the Lord in prayer!

Day 13

VITAMIN P

We all know the value of proper nutrition and many of us even take a daily vitamin to make sure that we are getting all we need. However, have you ever thought about the importance of spiritual nutrition? In fact, what might its basic component be?

In my experience, we MUST take at least one daily dose of Vitamin P. If we don't, we are like a car running on empty.

Have you figured out what Vitamin P is yet? Yes, it is prayer!

Prayer is an essential element that sustains our spiritual nutrition. Prayer keeps our soul healthy and maintains peace and direction from the inside out.

Prayer is a two-way avenue of communication. Between God and us.

Psychologists tell us that one of the most healthy ways to deal with stress, decision-making, or mending relationships is to talk it out. What better place to start than talking directly to the Creator and Lord of the Universe! THE One who knows us better than we know ourselves. Someone who can truly DO something about our troubles!

Of course, the other side of this communication equation involves God talking to us. Yes, prayer is more than us venting to God; prayer involves *listening* to God. It's the only way I know of to intake that precious vitamin "P!"

How does God talk to us? Yes, sometimes we do hear that still, small, voice that is truly audible in our thoughts. Sometimes we are directed to God's Word, which is a living, breathing document containing messages designed to guide us. The spiritual nutrition of vitamin "P" produces joy and gives us peace. First Peter 3:12 reminds us that, "...the eyes of the Lord are on the righteous and his ears are attentive to their prayer...."

Day 14

TUNE INTO SILENCE

Isaiah 30:15: "...in quietness and trust is your strength..."

The other day it occurred to me that very seldom do I cook, work, drive, or sit in silence. And let's face it, as busy parents at home and hard workers at our jobs, silence is sometimes a rare commodity! Kids love to play their loud music and yell over it on the phone to their friends. Muzak and "white noise" fill office buildings. For many of us, the first thing we do when getting into our car is to choose songs from our play list to connect to our Bluetooth. It leads me to ask the question: how much of what we listen to is really just useless static that takes our focus off of spending time with God?

You may remember a pop song that hit the charts many years ago called "Silence is Golden" (Crew/Gaudio). I think that there is some wisdom in that statement and that there can be value in occasionally tuning in to silence. Here are several positives that can result from an encounter with silence:

Tuning into silence allows our thoughts to become creative and constructive. If we are continually filling our brain waves with input from other sources, our energy is spent analyzing and assimilating that information. We barely have a chance to question the information when more input is given. This diverts us from the free-flow of natural output from within.

Tuning into silence gives us a rest from aggravations. Sometimes when noise pollution grates on me, I find that I grind my teeth, or feel a headache coming on. Silence is soothing in that it cleanses our ear palette and allows the flow of freethinking. In fact, I refuse to wear ear buds when working out or walking my four miles a day!

Finally, tuning into silence gives us an opportunity to hear God. If the noisiness around me distracts me too much, it fills my mind with messages from meaningless sources and squeezes out my recognition of God's voice. When I come to him in the beauty of silence, it gives me an opportunity to hear his heart and feel his love.

Day 15

UMBRELLA PRAYING

Today I want to talk about something I've coined "umbrella praying." First of all, let's picture a dark, cloudy day where the rain seems to stream in sheets around us. If we've forgotten our umbrella, we face the elements unprotected. We suffer the effects of the rain and are soon cold, soaked, and pretty miserable.

With an umbrella, especially those huge golf gizmos, we can withstand quite a down pour and still enjoy protection from the wet and cold.

Our prayers, in effect, act as umbrellas for those around us that we pray for. Think of the Father who daily lifts his requests to God concerning his family. In the spirit realm, can't you just see this prayer acting as an umbrella for his wife and children? Like an umbrella, this man's prayers cover his family and protects them from things in the spirit realm that can cause them grave harm.

What happens if I pray a half-hearted prayer that is laced with doubt? Well, the umbrella lifts a little, but only covers a part of my head and one shoulder. My face and toes aren't covered or protected. Soon, I'm squinting from the rain in my eyes, and shaking from the cold I feel as my clothes get drenched. I need the umbrella to reach higher and wider!

A prayer covering allows God's hand to protect us. I love the imagery of Exodus 33:22 when Moses asked to see God. God says, "When my glory passes by, I will put you in the cleft of the rock and cover you with my hand..." He did this to protect Moses. Galatians 3:27 tells us that when we are baptized in Christ, we have clothed ourselves in Christ.

Umbrella praying covers us with God's hand and allows us to be protected by wearing Christ as our garment.

Day 16

THINGS THAT HINDER PRAYER

Have you ever wondered if there are conditions for answered prayers? Well, the Bible is very clear that there ARE things that can hinder our prayers, not from being heard, but from being answered.

James 1:5-8 reads, "If any of you lacks wisdom, he should ask God, who gives generously to all without finding fault, and it will be given to him. But when he asks, he must believe and not doubt, because he who doubts is like a wave of the sea, blown and tossed by the wind. That man should not think he will receive anything from the Lord..."

Okay, so one condition for answered prayer is that we must believe and not doubt.

Here's another: Psalm 66:17-18 tells us "I cried out to him with my mouth; his praise was on my tongue. If I had cherished sin in my heart, the Lord would not have listened..."

Wow, there are several things here that give us insight as to how to receive answers to our prayers. First of all, the Psalmist poured out his heart to God and while he did that, he praised him. Here's the biggie, though: if we harbor sin, even in our hearts, God will not listen to us. Therefore, it is so important as we approach our prayer time with the Lord to confess and repent of any sin in our lives.

James 4:3 tells us "When you ask, you do not receive, because you ask with wrong motives, that you may spend what you get on your pleasures."

So, in just these three references we find the secret to things that hinder our prayers from being answered: we must not doubt, we must praise God and not harbor sin in our hearts, and we must pray with the right motives.

Day 17

SMOKE

If I were to ask you to answer this question and tell me the first thing that comes to mind, what would it be. Ready? Why pray?

Okay, now that you're formulating a quick answer, let's study a little about prayer from the book of Revelation, so of course, I'm going to direct you to Exodus 30!

In Exodus 30, God gives Moses a pattern and procedure from which to model God's dwelling place, the Tabernacle. In verse 7 He instructs Aaron, the High Priest, to burn a special blend formula of incense on the altar. Aaron is to burn it in the morning and evening, symbolic of burning throughout the generations.

God often provides a picture to us, explaining a spiritual truth through a physical example. Exodus begins to paint the picture of smoke rising from the incense to God. Now if we turn over to Psalm 141, verse 2, we read, "May my prayer be set before you like incense; may the lifting up of my hands be like the evening sacrifice."

We suddenly see a picture of our prayers rising to God like the smoke from the incense! It is a reminder that God loves the aroma of our prayers and hears them.

Now, let's turn to Revelation 5:8. Here we are given a vision of what it's like in the throne room of God. "And when he had taken (the scroll), the four living creatures and the twenty-four elders fell down before the Lamb. Each one had a harp and they were holding golden bowls full of incense, WHICH ARE THE PRAYERS OF THE SAINTS."

Imagine that! Apparently God receives all of our prayers and treasures them so much that He saves them! Our prayers are a special fragrance that rises to heaven. Why pray? Because God remembers and treasures our prayers!

Day 18

PUT YOUR MASK ON FIRST

Matthew 6:33: "But seek first his kingdom and his righteousness and all these things will be given to you as well."

If you've ever flown, you probably know the safety speech by heart! "Fasten your seatbelts, make sure that your seats are fully upright with tray tables in a locked position..." and on the instructions drone.

One instruction, however, really has in it a life lesson for those of us who are busy parents, working men and women, or volunteers. They mention that if the cabin should loose air pressure, an oxygen mask will automatically drop from the ceiling. Then they suggest that if you are traveling with someone who needs your assistance that you put your own mask on FIRST, BEFORE helping those around you.

Oxygen is a life-giving, life-preserving resource. Without it, we die. Just think what would happen to us if we WERE in a depressurized cabin and went about tending to everybody else first, making sure their masks were in place: "Are you comfy...can I get you a pillow or blanket? Some water?" We soon would run out of air and collapse—so busy helping others that we failed to take care of ourselves.

How many times do we tend to the needs and demands of those around us at the expense of our own physical and spiritual well-being? Yet this simple flight instruction holds great wisdom for us. We can only have the life in us, the strength, and the stamina to assist those around us, if we ourselves are filled with a sufficient amount of God's life force.

This means that we need to take time for us! Daily prayer and Bible reading; a 15-minute walk around the neighborhood; letting voice mail take messages; reading a magazine or good book; learning to say "no." Be sure to put your own oxygen mask on first. Only then will you be able to assist those around you....

Day 19

THE BLESSING

Up until modern history, two things were coveted from one generation to another: obviously, the material inheritance one would receive, but for many years, in addition to the material heritage, children sought from their parents a blessing.

There are many children who, long after their parents are gone, continue to mourn the fact that even though they received a material inheritance, they never received the blessing—the love, acceptance, and respect—from the father.

In much the same way, the story of Jacob exemplifies the insatiable hunger to receive his father's blessing; not just his biological father, but his heavenly father.

Genesis 25 records how Jacob deceitfully bought the birthright from his twin brother Esau, and Genesis 27 records how he tricked his father, Isaac, into also giving him the blessing. Both of these were entitled to Esau who was the firstborn.

Genesis 32, then reveals to us that Jacob must have finally come to the correct conclusion that a true blessing can only be granted by God the Father. After having run away from the trouble he created most of his life, he finally decides to return to the Promised Land in hopes of repenting to Esau and making peace.

Genesis 32:24 begins the passage where Jacob wrestles with a "man" all night. Scripture reveals that this "man" was God in the form of an angel. As we read this story, we get the sense that it is Jacob who continues in the fight because he finally yells out to the Angel, "I will not let you go until you have blessed me!"

In the process, Jacob's hip socket was broken and apparently he limped the rest of his life. Here are three key things we can extract from this story:

First of all, it is God who gives the blessing. When we seek the blessing from anyone else, it will not satisfy.

Second, God uses our brokenness to make us stronger. Did you know that a bone becomes strongest in the place where a break has healed? So it is with us when we come before the Lord, broken and surrendered. He makes us stronger.

Finally, when God blesses us, it changes us. Not only did Jacob walk differently, as a daily reminder of his encounter with God, but God gave him a new name: Israel.

We are not to wrestle *against* God, but *with* Him. He allows us this privilege so that we can become stronger and forever changed.

PRAYER UNLEASHES POWER!

EM Bounds was a theologian who lived in the 19th century who dedicated his life to the study of prayer. He wrote 11 books on prayer, but only two were published. The truths that he reveals are just as relevant today since the power of prayer is timeless. In "The Necessity of Prayer" he wrote: "The prayers of God's saints are the capital stock in heaven by which Christ carries on His great work on earth...Earth is changed, revolutionized and angels move on more powerful, more rapid wing, and God's policy is shaped as the prayers are more numerous, more efficient."

In other words, our prayers become the power source for spiritual activity in God's kingdom, much like an electrical socket that supplies the needed current for an appliance to work. Or, our prayers are much like the fuel we place in our gas tank, which ignites energy for the vehicle to run on.

EM Bounds claims that PRAYER PUTS GOD IN FULL FORCE IN THE WORLD!

Yes, God is all powerful, but in a sense, it is prayer that totally unbinds His hands so that He can shape and mold his policies most efficiently in the world. In the spiritual battle that is raging all around us, what weapon can we use? It doesn't help to raise our fists and get angry. Our greatest weapon is prayer and the Word of God.

When you are wanting to unleash the heavenly powers and fight spiritual warfare, let me suggest this prayer: "In the name of Jesus and by his blood I claim that your Word is true. You have told us that you will never leave us nor forsake us and that the battle is yours not ours. Therefore, unleash your mighty angels against the Evil One and protect us from harm. I pray this in the name of the Father, the Son, and the Holy Spirit! Amen!"

Day 21

PRAYING FOR OTHERS

The Bible encourages us to pray for each other. James 5:16 says, "Therefore confess your sins to each other and pray for each other so that you may be healed." A logical conclusion is that we receive spiritual and emotional healing by doing so.

Ezekiel 22:30 reads "I looked for a man among them who would build up the wall and stand before me in the gap on behalf of the land...." This is a beautiful word picture of how sin separates us from a Holy God...therefore creating a huge chasm between us. God looks for people who are willing to stand in that gap on behalf of others—even those who are less than lovable!

In fact, Jesus in Matthew 5:44 tells us that we are to pray even for those who ridicule and threaten us: "But I tell you: Love your enemies and pray for those who persecute you..."

We are to also pray for those who mistreat us: Luke 6:28 says, "Bless those who curse you, pray for those who mistreat you."

These are hard things for us since our natural instinct is to hate and curse those who persecute and mistreat us. But, we must remember that the battle we fight is in the spirit realm and that praying for our enemies allows us to forgive and love them—emotions that lead to our health and healing, not bitter resentment that eats at us from the inside out.

And, here's the most comforting truth about intercessory prayer. The Holy Spirit Himself intercedes on our behalf.

Romans 8:26-27 says "In the same way, the Spirit helps us in our weakness. We do not know what we ought to pray for, but the Spirit himself intercedes for us with groans that words cannot express."

Day 22

PLAN TO PRAY

One of the greatest laments I hear from people when I travel and speak is that they just can't get "into" prayer. They ask me how they can do better at the art of praying.

My answer always is, to make prayer a part of your daily routine, you've got to plan for it, just like you would a doctor's appointment or important meeting.

If you keep a daily calendar, look ahead to the next week and pencil in an appointment with Jesus as your schedule allows. Perhaps you get the kids on the school bus and by 8:30 a.m. feel you can spend until 9:00 praying and reading the Scriptures. Perhaps, like me, you're a night owl and like to crawl in bed early with your Bible and an attitude of prayer. No matter when or where, it's important that this becomes time we consciously set aside to spend with our Lord!

Next, you may want to keep a prayer journal. Date it and list things you want to pray for. You may even write out your prayers to God. Either way, your faith will grow when you look back upon your last weeks and months of prayers and see how God has performed miracles!

Finally, if you need a format from which to begin praying, try the "ACTS" method. This is an acronym for praying in these areas:

Adoration: Adore God.

Confession: Confess your sins and forgive others.

Thanksgiving: Thank him for answered prayer and all the blessings that you enjoy.

Supplication: Make your requests known.

There will be times when God answers your prayers through astounding miracles, or he may quietly guide you with peace and confidence. Regardless of what the answer and how it is revealed, we know that there is power when we pray!

Day 23

MUSTARD SEED

He made his way into the kitchen, whistling and opening one cupboard after another until he discovered the spices. This ought to be interesting, I thought. The only things my husband can cook are scrambled eggs and French toast.

After lifting several containers and reading the labels, apparently he found what he was looking for. He opened the cap and tapped something into his hand. "Got any scotch tape?"

"In my office."

He scuffed through the living room into my office and tore off a piece of tape. On his way back through the living room, he stopped before me and held out the tape to show me he had doubled it over to hold a small mustard seed. He then quoted Jesus' words found in Matthew 17:20: "...if you have faith as small as a mustard seed, you can say to this mountain, 'Move from here to there' and it will move. Nothing will be impossible for you."

That small piece of tape with the mustard seed in it is still attached to the inside of my husband's brief case as a constant reminder of the fact that with just the smallest amount of faith "nothing will be impossible" for us.

Faith has to do with what we believe and put our trust in. When we make a commitment to Jesus Christ, our faith may seem small and weak, but if we remember the mustard seed, we can take heart. You see, in Jesus' time, the mustard seed was the smallest seed known. Yet when planted on fertile ground and given the right atmosphere, it could grow to over 15 feet tall! We may possess just the smallest amount of faith, but when we place it in the power and presence of Jesus Christ, our faith begins to grow.

Day 24

MIST

It seems that a prevalent issue we deal with is guilt.

We feel guilty that the house isn't all picked up and clean all of the time. We feel guilty that we said "No" to a volunteer cause. We feel guilty because we get sick and have to rest. We feel guilty that we worked so hard and didn't get that promotion, or didn't get the bonus we felt we had coming. We even feel guilty when our kids make bad decisions.

Even more prevalent is the guilt we suffer regarding our past sins. Yes, we have confessed and repented, yet the memories still haunt us. Can God REALLY forgive us?

Once we have entered into a relationship with Jesus Christ and asked for forgiveness, the Bible tells us that our sin is as far as the East is from the West and God remembers it no more. Yet, one of Satan's tricks is to continually deceive us into thinking that we're just not good enough and have not done enough good works to be able to be forgiven.

Isaiah 44 gives us a beautiful analogy about our past sin. Verse 21 says, "O Israel, I will not forget you. I have swept away your offenses like a cloud, your sins like the morning mist."

Think of this image and picture in your mind a spray bottle filled with water. If we hold up the bottle and spray it into the air, what happens? The water escapes the bottle as a mist, and then it DISAPPEARS! Yes! Just like that, when we come before God and ask to be forgiven of our sin, it is as though our sin is a vapor mist that evaporates and is seen nor more. We can't feel guilty about something that doesn't exist!

INSTRUCTIONS ON PRAYER

The Bible guides us in our daily walk with Christ and gives us instructions on praying. Today we're going to look up a few verses that instruct us as to the right way to pray.

Matthew 6:5-6 reveal to us that praying should often be a private matter where we humble ourselves alone before God. Jesus said, "And when you pray, do not be like the hypocrites, for they love to pray standing in the synagogues and on the street corners to be seen by men. I tell you the truth, they have received their reward in full. But when you pray, go into your room, close the door and pray to your Father, who is unseen. Then your Father, who sees what is done in secret will reward you."

In Luke 6:27-28 Jesus teaches us who to pray for, and sometimes this is not easy! He says, "...Love you enemies, do good to those who hurt you, bless those who curse you, pray for those who mistreat you." Oh, and don't we know just how to pray for those who hurt us? Well, it seems what Jesus has in mind is for us to pray for the salvation of our enemies, doesn't it? And when we are praying for those who mistreat us, it's a little easier to forgive and not allow the hurt to fester. Each soul is precious in God's eyes and he wants us to want them to know his love and forgiveness—no matter what they've done to us.

So, we are instructed to spend time alone with God and while there to pray for those who hurt and mistreat us. Through prayer we can release them to God and in doing that, he will release us from any stress from it.

Day 26

IN THE FULLNESS OF TIME

Psalm 62:8: "Trust in him at all times, O people; pour out your hearts to him, for God is our refuge."

Exodus 24:12 continues the incredible progression of God's instruction to Moses to build a Tabernacle so that He can dwell among His people.

The Lord says to Moses: "Come up to me on the mountain and stay here—and I will give you the tablets of stone, with the law and commands I have written for their instruction." This passage takes us about one minute to read and then chapter 25 begins with all of the instructions for building the Tabernacle. Sounds pretty succinct.

A closer analysis, however, reveals that God did not immediately speak to Moses when he "came up" to the mountain. In fact, verse 16 says that "For six days the cloud covered the mountain, and on the seventh day the Lord called to Moses from within the cloud."

Okay, so here's Moses waiting for God to speak: on day one: we see him practicing his golf swing; day two, whistling bird calls: day three, a game of pick up sticks: day four, playing marbles with small stones: day five, using the stones to hit a small target with his sling shot; day six, "hmmm, that cloud kinda looks like a dragon...." FINALLY on day seven—God speaks!

I'm just kidding about what Moses did while he waited. It's probable that he was praying, purifying his own heart and making intercession for the Children of Israel. And when does God finally speak? In the fullness of time! The seventh day represents the perfect number and God always responds at the perfect time. It was also the day He rested during creation and the day He asked the Children of Israel to set aside as their Sabbath.

There may be times when God calls us up to his mountain to speak to us and we think he is delayed or has stood us up. But like Moses, we must "stay here" and wait for God to speak in the fullness of time—His time.

Day 27
THE TRUTH ABOUT SATAN

Have you ever wondered where Satan came from and why he is so evil?

Isaiah 14:12-15 and Ezekiel 28:11-19 paint for us a picture of Satan's original position and the reasons for the loss of that position. He was originally one of the most exalted angelic beings that God ever created, yet he became proud and overly-ambitious to the point where he determined to take over God's throne for himself. Revelation 12:3-4 reveals that Satan convinced one-third of the angelic host to join with him in this rebellion.

Satan is clever and intelligent, yet does not possess limitless power as does God. He is subject to God's restrictions. There are times when Satan has been allowed to afflict God's people. In Job 1:7-12, Satan is restricted by God's limits as to how far he can test Job's faithfulness. Luke 13:16 reveals that Satan had bound a woman through illness. Daniel's answer to prayer was delayed by 21 days in Daniel 10. Yet in each case, God was and is the ultimate victor and receives glory and honor through the victory.

Of the various methods Satan uses to manipulate and deceive us, the use of temptation is his greatest. He sometimes uses direct suggestion as he did with Judas Iscariot. Other times, he tempts us through our own weaknesses or lack of self-control. Satan tries to imitate God's power so we will be deceived.

How can we keep from being tempted and deceived? First John 4:1-4 tells us to "test the spirits." Then we can discern God's truth from Satan's lies.

Furthermore, we have victory over sin because of what Jesus accomplished on the cross. For a time, it looked as if Satan had won, but when Christ rose from the grave, he defeated Satan for all eternity.

Day 28

BENEFITS OF PRAYER

We know we are supposed to pray and really WANT to pray, but sometimes just don't know why. Lucky for us, the Bible gives us clear directions! In fact, there are many benefits to praying!

Matthew 26:41 tells us that praying is a way to avoid temptation. Jesus said to his disciples: "Watch and pray that you will not fall into temptation. The spirit is willing, but the body is weak."

James 4:8 tells us to "Come near to God and he will come near to you." When people complain that they just aren't very close to God anymore, uh, who moved?

Isaiah 40:29 assures us that what we need, God will supply: "He gives strength to the weary and increases the power of the weak." On down to verse 31 it continues: "...but those who hope in the Lord will renew their strength. They will soar on wings like eagles, they will run and not grow weary, they will walk and not be faint." All of these blessings are available to us through the avenue of prayer!

Finally, one of the most astounding benefits we realize through the avenue of prayer is available to us as Jesus described in John 3:16: "...that whosoever believes in him will not perish but have eternal life."

So, it is through prayer that we can avoid temptation to sin; it is through prayer that God will come near to us, it is through prayer that we are given supernatural power to run life's race and not grow weary, and it is through prayer that we receive eternal life. Thank you, Lord, for hearing our prayers!

Day 29

GO TO THE MOUNTAIN

Matthew 6:6: "But when you pray, go into your room, close the door and pray to your Father, who is unseen."

Jesus surely dealt with a plate full of stress between his teaching ministry, directing his disciples, and watching out for the needs of his family as the oldest male—not to mention that towards the end of his life, there were many who wanted to kill him! So how did he handle the stress?

Mark 6:46 and many other Bible references reveal that often "He went up to the mountain to pray." Even Jesus, who was God incarnate, found it necessary to spend time in prayer!

Think of the wisdom in this piece of advice. First of all, it was probably a little bit of a trek to get to his "spot" on the mountain, so he enjoyed some much-needed exercise. We know now that walking is a great way to handle stress!

Next, he probably chose a spot that he really enjoyed. Just think, it may have had a beautiful view and carried the aroma of wild flowers... what we now would term aroma therapy! It would be smart for you and me to also choose a pleasant place set aside just for prayer that in the same way warms and soothes us.

It appears that Jesus went alone to this place of prayer. This way he had no interruptions or distractions to take his focus off of prayer. If you and I can find a quiet place alone for prayer (leaving the cell phone and lap top behind for a while), we also have the same opportunity that Jesus did to communicate clearly and sincerely with God the Father.

Psychologists tell us that one of the best ways to deal with stress is to talk it out. What better way to unload a burden then to lay it at the feet of the One who is the God of all comfort.

Day 30

DELAYED ANSWERS

We live in a microwave culture where we expect immediate gratification and instant replays. We now even term "next day mail" as the snail mail due to our dependence upon E-mail, Texting, Twitter, and Instagram. Any delay becomes irritating, frustrating and just plain annoying.

In our way of thinking, delays cost us money and waste our precious time. Delays also discourage us from pressing on and being persistent.

How do you react when your plans or prayers are delayed from being implemented and answered? Do you get angry with God? Do you get impatient? Do you give up?

Daniel faced just such a delay in Daniel 10:13 when one of his fervent prayers was not immediately answered. How did he respond? Did he pout and stomp around like a spoiled child? Did he doubt God and give up?

No way! The word tells us that he diligently persisted in prayer until the answer finally came.

This particular delay was actually due to warfare in the spirit realm. When the angel Gabriel finally appears to Daniel with God's answer, he reveals that the spiritual warfare delayed him 21 days!

The encouraging aspect of this story is that although the answer was delayed, the request had been immediately heard by God. What a comfort to know that as soon as we pray to God, he hears us! This delay did not discourage Daniel or deter him from persistently and faithfully worshipping his God. And God's delays should not keep us from diligently seeking him.

While it may take time for answers to come, we can be assured that God does hear us and has the answers! Our only duty then, is to make sure we continue to believe that the answer is on the way and wait patiently for it to come to us!

Day 31
TESTING

If I say the word "test," what will naturally come to most of us is a feeling of dread. We either remember what it was (or is) to cram for an exam, or we think about the things that happen to us in life that test our patience, our endurance, and our faithfulness.

When you face a test do you turn away from it or do you trust God? Do you run from it or walk to it? Do you try to avoid the pain or allow it to purify you in some way?

When I think of the purification process, I often think of gold and the refinement of its properties. It is one of the few metals that can be used in its pure state without smelting. It is purified by a very hot fire which eliminates the dross or unnecessary elements that might be found in it.

In its pure state, gold exhibits two qualities that are also paralleled by our testing in the spiritual realm: it is malleable or flexible, and it cannot be tarnished.

When a test puts us to the fire and we put our trust in God for the result, we can be encouraged that good will always come of it. First, the testing will allow us to become pure before the Lord, which is the only way we can be in His presence. It will then allow us to be bended and molded so that we can be likened into the image of Christ. Finally, it will keep us from being tainted or tarnished by un-pure elements that face and surround us each day.

Okay, God, turn the heat up and allow us to echo Job's words in Job 23:10: "...when he has tested me, I will come forth as gold."

Day 32
HUMILITY

Matthew 18:4: "Therefore, whoever humbles himself like this child is the greatest in the kingdom of heaven."

The Bible has much to say about the virtue of humility. Numbers 12:3 records that Moses was the most humble man on the face of the earth. And look what God was able to do through him!

Proverbs 11:2 says, "When pride comes, then comes disgrace, but with humility comes wisdom."

Matthew 11:28-29 records some of my most favorite words of encouragement from Jesus: "Come to me, all you who are weary and burdened, and I will give you rest. Take my yoke upon you and learn from me, for I am gentle and humble in heart, and you will find rest for your souls."

Humility can be defined as "one without pride; performing an act of submission."

There are several undeniable marks of a person with humility. That person is:

- teachable and knows how to receive instruction.
- approachable and follows Jesus' example of "come unto me."
- obedient, with outward actions reflecting inner motives.
- submissive, placing others before and above him/herself.
- gentle, and this means that in his/her meekness they may be "velvet over steel," but have a softness that reflects humility.
- prayerful. Openly confessing that we cannot make it on own but need to take upon us the yoke of Jesus Christ.

Humility is the ability to acknowledge who we are in relationship to God. I Peter 5:5-6 says it this way: "...clothe yourselves in humility.... Humble yourselves, therefore, under God's mighty hand, that he may lift you up in due time." The greatest voice that ever spoke humbled himself "and became obedient to death—even death on a cross." (Philippians 2:8)

Day 33

THE BEST MEDICINE

How do you stay up when life gets you down?

There is no question that we will likely always have circumstances that trouble us and drag us down, so what can we do to keep things in perspective?

If you can remember the Reader's Digests, one of their columns was: "Laughter is the best medicine."

In fact, researchers have found that when we laugh, we actually produce endorphins that promote health and well-being to our bodies and that help to stabilize our emotions. It stands to reason that if we are fit physically and emotionally, we will be better suited to face the "down" times in our lives.

Have you even ever considered that the people you hang out with might have those personality types that are rather melancholy, so they are "down" people? If that is the case, while you don't want to necessarily "dump" them, you may want to seek out those with more positive outlooks who possess fun senses of humor!

And here's a tip: on those days when you just need a little pick-me-up and you have the time: visit the card section at your local gift shop. Sometimes I just have to have a "laugh out loud" moment in the aisle because the jokes are that good!

Proverbs 15:30: "A cheerful look brings joy to the heart."

Proverbs 17:22: "A cheerful heart is good medicine."

Proverbs 16:24: "Pleasant words are a honeycomb, sweet to the soul and a healing to the bones."

It is said that it takes more muscles and energy to frown than to smile, so as the saying goes, "put on a happy face!"

POSITIVE SELF-TALK

Psychologists tell us that one way to successfully handle stress and the disappointment that life sometimes heaps on us is to practice positive self-talk. Remember that little chorus we sang in Sunday School? "Count your blessings name them one by one, count your blessings see what God has done" (Reginald Morgan). This little chorus teaches us great theology.

A few years ago when my husband lost his job, I watched him sink further and further into a depressed funk. The bills were piling up as high as the employment rejection letters. One thing that helped us put the situation in perspective was counting our blessings through positive self-talk. We didn't have a job or any money and we were close to losing our home and sometimes going without food, but our children were both healthy. We had a circle of loving family and friends. There was hope for the future.

King David is one of the greatest examples of a person who practiced positive self-talk. Listen to some of the statements he makes in the Psalms that gave him hope and courage to face the future: "The earth is the Lord's and everything in it" (Ps 24:1). "The Lord is a refuge for the oppressed, a stronghold in times of trouble" (Ps 9:9). "I call on you Lord for you will answer me" (Ps 17:6). "The Lord is my strength and shield; my heart trusts in him, and I am helped" (Ps 28:7). "But the plans of the Lord stand firm forever, the purposes of his heart through all generations" (Ps 33:11). "Even though I walk through the valley of the shadow of death, I will fear no evil for you are with me" Ps 23:4).

The Bible is FILLED with verses that can encourage and inspire us, if we just take the time to look. Here are some of my favorites, just from the book of Matthew:

Matthew 5:11: "Blessed are you when people insult you, persecute you and falsely say all kinds of evil against you because of me. Rejoice and be glad, because great is your reward in heaven...."

Matthew 6:34: "Therefore do not worry about tomorrow, for tomorrow will worry about itself. Each day has enough trouble of its own."

Matthew 10: 19: "...do not worry about what to say or how to say it. At that time you will be given what to say...."

Matthew 11:28: "Come to me, all you who are weary and burdened and I will give your rest."

Matthew 19:26: "...with God all things are possible."

Matthew 21:22: "If you believe, you will receive whatever you ask for in prayer."

Matthew 23:39: "...Blessed is he who comes in the name of the Lord."

Matthew 24:35: "Heaven and earth will pass away, but my words will never pass away."

Matthew 28:17: "All authority in heaven and on earth has been given to me."

And finally, the very last words from the book of Matthew are from Jesus: "And surely I am with you always, to the very end of the age."

In addition, Second Corinthians 1:3 tells us that God is "the God of all comfort." Verse 10 tells us that "he will deliver us!" Chapter 4 verse 8 says, "We are hard pressed on every side, but not crushed; perplexed, but not in despair; persecuted, but not abandoned; struck down, but not destroyed."

Chapter 7:6 tells us that God "comforts the downcast."

Ephesians 2:14 reminds us that God "himself is our peace."

Philippians 1:6 says, "He who began a good work in you will carry it on to completion...."

Philippians 1:21: "For to live is Christ; to die is gain."

Philippians 4:19: "And my God will meet all your needs according to his glorious riches in Christ Jesus."

James 5:11: "The Lord is full of compassion and mercy."

John 16:24: "Ask and you will receive, and your joy will be complete."

John 10:10: "I have come that you may have life, and have it to the full."

Finally, Jesus' own words in John 14:27 encourage us that "Peace I leave with you; my peace I give you. I do not give to you as the world gives. Do not let your hearts be troubled and do not be afraid." And John 16:33: "In this world you will have trouble. But take heart! I have overcome the world."

Aren't these wonderful reminders of how faithful our God is!

Maybe you will want to book mark this page to return to and revisit these Scriptures whenever you are discouraged!

Day 35

GIVE

In Luke 6:38, Jesus tells us to "give, and it will be given to you. A good measure, pressed down, shaken together and running over...."

Have you ever noticed that stingy, greedy people are the most depressed, anxious, and miserable people to be around? The very thing they grope and scrape for—the thing they think will make them happy—is actually the thing that torments them. And why? Because there is no joy in keeping blessings to ourselves!

The author of Ecclesiastes makes this point repeatedly throughout his teaching. The theme is that everything in life is meaningless, if not centered around the will and purposes of God. Chapter 11, verses 1 and 2 contain a familiar adage: "Cast your bread upon the waters, for after many days you will find it. Give portions to seven, yes to eight, for you do not know what disaster may come upon the land."

All of these instructions encourage us to give liberally, take a few risks, and divide our plenty with others when we have it, for we do not know what tomorrow may bring.

A millionaire who went bankrupt was interviewed and asked if he resented the fact that he had given so much of his money away to the church when he had it. He responded that the giving is what completed his life and gave him so much joy. It wasn't long after the interview that he started another company and made back his fortune—only to be able to give it away again!

"Give, and it will be given to you. A good measure, pressed down, shaken together and running over...."

Day 36

KINDNESS

Have you ever noticed that kindness lends beauty to the one who displays it? There's just something about being with a kind person that inspires us to mirror that beauty.

Proverbs 11:14 tells us that "A kindhearted woman gains respect, but ruthless men only gain wealth." Isn't that interesting? Respect from kindness is valued far beyond gaining wealth!

In the corporate world where I lived for years, I witnessed so-called leaders—who were given titles and positions—who couldn't understand why their employees disliked them. They tried motivating from using threats, and being unkind, then could not understand why they couldn't get results. Proverbs tells us that respect is gained through being kind-hearted. It's much more motivating to work with/ for someone who is kind and helpful. In fact, a survey was once taken that asked if an employee would rather have a pay raise and work for an unkind boss, or have less take-home but work in a friendly environment. It was unanimous. Work with kindness.

What are some of the ways that we can show kindness? I would like to suggest that one of the best ways is to use that universal language, the smile! See, even when you just hear the word, didn't a smile sweep over your face?

Another way we can show kindness is to give words of encouragement. I don't know about you, but there are days when I open my email up and see who has sent me something and I either cringe, knowing I'm going to get lambasted for something, or I can't wait to open up the words of encouragement I know I will hear from the next person. Proverbs 12:25 says, "An anxious heart weighs a man down, but a kind word cheers him up."

Proverbs 14:31 reminds us that "He who oppresses the poor shows contempt for their Maker, but whoever is kind to the needy honors God." Again, there is joy in giving.

Acts of kindness, such as smiling, giving words of encouragement, and lending a helping hand to those in need, reflect character traits of God. Since we are made in His image, let's choose to be kind!

Day 37
FORGIVENESS

Colossians 3:13 reads, "Bear with each other and forgive whatever grievances you may have against one another. Forgive as the Lord forgave you."

When I read this, I think of the familiar adage that says, "Grin and bear it!" Yes, there are certain encounters with others that we simply grit our teeth and patiently bear the unpleasantness, but this is clearly what we are commanded to do.

The Apostle Paul tells us that we must forgive whatever grievances we have against each other. And I want to point out that the Scripture does not say that we must first be asked for forgiveness! We must grant that person forgiveness for that grievance whether they have apologized or not.

But the most profound aspect of this verse is that we are told to forgive as the Lord forgives us. And how does the Lord forgive us? John 3:16 reminds us that God loved us so much that he gave his life for us. And how many times are we commanded to forgive an infraction? In Matthew 18:21, Jesus says, seventy times seven—which implies, an infinite amount.

The most sobering thought on forgiveness, however, is taught by Jesus in Matthew 6:14: "For if you forgive men when they sin against you, your heavenly Father will also forgive you. But if you do not forgive men their sins, your Father will not forgive your sins."

Don't let anything keep God from forgiving your sins. If there is someone in your life who has sinned against you, forgive them! Even if they have not asked for forgiveness, forgive them! If they've asked for forgiveness and you've refused to reconcile, you are in danger of losing God's forgiveness.

Day 38

THOUGHTS

We live in a culture now where so many do not adhere to a standard, especially a biblical standard. There really are absolutes. God is absolute and deliberately gives guidance on what "right thinking" and proper behavior is. One has to only begin reading in Exodus 20 when God wrote what we now call the Ten Commandments and gave to Moses. Then if you flip over to Leviticus, and Deuteronomy, you will see additional laws and the repetition of those laws. Why? Well, here is a nation who had been enslaved for 400 years. They had no sense of government, and with no laws, they were bickering amongst themselves and driving poor Moses crazy trying to resolve disputes.

All that to say, yes, there is a standard that God imposes so that we will be a "right-thinking" people!

Right thinking involves aligning our thoughts with those of Christ. You see, even though we have been created with a built-in conscience, we still stray in our thought process if it isn't aligned with Christ.

I was watching Larry King Live one night when country star Charlie Daniels was being interviewed. You may know that he maintains a strong Christian faith, which came up in the conversation. When asked what he thought about a certain, rather, politically delicate topic, he responded to Mr. King, "Hey, it doesn't matter what I think about this. I'm just telling you what God thinks!"

I thought that was a great response! Our thinking needs to be based upon God's thinking. When we place the foundation of our beliefs on the Lord, our thoughts will wander to those principles, rather than to the confusion of the many beliefs we are asked to consider each day.

Ralph Waldo Emerson once said, "A man is what he thinks about all day long." Our thoughts fashion our state of mind—which includes attitudes and mental well-being. Our thought process also shapes our behavior. How many affairs have resulted from pondering and thinking about that possibility for a long period of time beforehand? Our thoughts can even determine our state of physical well-being. Worry often results in high blood pressure and can create unhealthy chemicals in the blood stream.

However, pondering God's promises and our hope for eternal life produce in us a calm and peace that the world just doesn't understand. It all begins with our thoughts.

Day 39
WHOLESOME THINKING

In Peter's second letter, he talks about the fact that he wrote it to "stimulate you to wholesome thinking." I've jotted down several things that I consider to be in the category of wholesome thinking.

First of all, wholesome thinking involves putting others before ourselves. Romans 21:3 warns us not to "think of yourself more highly than you ought...." Philippians 2:3 admonishes us to "do nothing out of vain conceit, but in humility consider others better than yourselves." In Luke 10:27, even Jesus addressed this issue when he commanded "love your neighbor as yourself." When we consider the importance of others, we are inclined to follow the golden rule: "treat others as you would like to be treated."

Another aspect of wholesome thinking involves the ability to see the good in others. Yes, that co-worker is very cranky and obnoxious in her attention to detail and perfectionism and it can drive one up the wall, so to speak. However, it is her ability to catch mistakes and produce a product of excellence that allows her to be an asset to your organization. Wholesome thinking means that we take note of her positive qualities.

Wholesome thinking also involves pondering things that are wholesome. We do this through reading God's Word and praying. Our spiritual nutritional intake must include wholesome thoughts if we are to be heart-healthy. Philippians 4:8 says it so succinctly: "Whatever is true, whatever is noble, whatever is right, whatever is pure, whatever is lovely, whatever is admirable—if anything is excellent or praiseworthy—think about such things."

Day 40
HONESTY

Perhaps I'm naïve because I take people at face value and accept what they say as reflecting how they feel or that they are telling the truth. Nothing is more frustrating than to walk away from a conversation thinking the person feels one way, then have it come back around somehow that they didn't really mean what they said! I'd rather have it straight!

In Matthew 5:37, Jesus is just ending a teaching on this very thing. He says, "Let your 'yes' be 'yes' and your 'no,' 'no.' Anything beyond this comes from the evil one."

James 5:12 deals with the same issue. He says, "…do not swear—not by heaven or by earth or by anything else. Let your 'Yes' be 'Yes,' and your 'No,' be 'No,' or you will be condemned." James is condemning the flippant use of God's name to guarantee the truth of what is spoken. Our word should be enough!

If we could all get in the habit of telling the truth straight out, what a different world it would be! Legal contracts would be at a minimum because our words and a handshake would seal the deal. We wouldn't play those silly games where we just give the answer someone wants to hear, knowing that we don't have any intention of following through. Problems would surface and be resolved quickly if we kindly voiced our concern at the very beginning and allowed that opposition to formulate the answer.

One of my friend's daughters is an attorney. She loved the courtroom, but ethically could not defend someone she knew to be guilty. She quit her job and became a veterinarian! She wanted her yes to be yes and her no to be no and was willing to put her career on the line to live out God's standards. What an example of honesty to herself for admitting the truth of her situation. And isn't she the one you would want to attend to your sick pet? You know that she's going to be honest about the diagnosis and treatment. Oh, that there were more like her in the world!

Day 41

THE WAIT ROOM

One of my dear prayer partners gives some insight into the weight room. You know all about that place: it's a part of our physical workout designed for resistance training so that our muscles will become conditioned and strong. It's a place that takes time, patience, and consistency in order for us to see results. Sometimes it requires us to lift a heavy burden in order to grow and change.

Well, sometimes God puts us through a similar spiritual workout and it takes place in the wait (W A I T) room. This is the place where God tests our faith by allowing us to spend time waiting on Him for direction, answers, and peace.

As I look back on my life, I certainly can visualize several times when we have been placed in the wait room—waiting upon God to reveal his truths and purpose for our lives. In fact, we were in one such wait room for almost four years, when my husband lost a lucrative job and was not able to find full-time employment. Yes, he picked up some consulting work and I found a part-time teaching job, but it seemed like a long wait for something to open up for him. But, it was in that wait room that we grew stronger, got closer, and learned things about God we would not have learned any other way.

The wait room forced us to be totally dependent upon God and to submit to the plan he had for our lives. The miraculous experiences in our wait room included provision for our needs in the most unexpected shapes and forms. We could greet each new day with anticipation and marvel as we saw God work in our lives.

The wait room conditions our faith and makes it strong; the wait room forces us into resistance training where we come up against our enemy with confidence; the wait room insures that we have the endurance to run the race with confidence and joy.

Day 42

THE BURNING HUT

Roger Knapp shares this illustration: The only survivor of a shipwreck was washed up on a small, uninhabited island. He prayed feverishly for God to rescue him, and every day he scanned the horizon for help, but none seemed forth coming. Exhausted, he eventually managed to build a little hut out of driftwood to protect himself from the elements, and to store his few possessions.

But then one day, after scavenging for food, he arrived home to find his little hut in flames, the smoke rolling up to the sky. The worst had happened; everything was lost. He was stunned with grief and anger. "God, how could you do this to me!" he cried.

Early the next day, however, he was awakened by the sound of a ship that was approaching the island. It had come to rescue him. "How did you know I was here?" asked the weary man of his rescuers. "We saw your smoke signal," they replied.

It is easy to get discouraged when things are going bad. But we shouldn't lose heart, because God is at work in our lives, even in the midst of pain and suffering. Remember, next time your little hut is burning to the ground, it just may be a smoke signal that summons the grace of God.

Day 43
STEPPING STONES

I'm getting old enough to look back on my life journey and see how God has guided my steps, like stepping stones, from one stone to another, crossing from this side of life's river onto heaven's shore.

At the time, I had no idea which stone to step onto next. It looked like an endless maze leading no place in the dark! However, as I look back on the path I've followed, I can see how each of the steps I trusted God to guide me to has been the life journey he planned for me.

For one thing, I believe it is no mistake what family we are born into. Mine was musical and filled with school teachers and church leaders. Each class, lesson, performance, and relationship have been stepping stones for me to grow closer to the Lord and prepare for ministry.

God did not waste a five-year desert of my life teaching high school under the administration of an atheist principal who took every opportunity to harass, criticize, and show contempt to my faith. This became a stepping stone in learning how to live and defend my faith— and grow as a teacher.

God used the unemployment of my husband to force us to step out on another stone that required relocating our family to a new city. This move has been the impetus behind writing and recording music, authoring books and developing a women's ministry.

Like you, I have no idea what my next stepping stone will be, but I know God will reveal it and help me step out in faith on this journey. Proverbs 20:24 reminds us that "A man's steps are directed by the Lord."

Day 44
REPENTANCE

If you can visualize that moment when the larva bursts forth as a beautiful butterfly, that somewhat illustrates the idea of repentance. A metamorphosis takes place when there is a change of shape. The word repentance comes from the same root word in the Greek: metanoia. Repentance refers to a change of mind.

True repentance results in more than just a change of mind, however. Repentance takes place when there is a change of life direction and our behavior. It's not enough that we believe in Jesus and the forgiveness of sins (even the demons do that), our choices and decisions must now reflect that we have turned from our wicked ways to do God's will. Repentance reflects a transformation within us that spills over to our actions.

In Romans 12:2, Paul tells us that we can be "transformed by the renewing of your mind..." Changed behavior begins in the mind. Our actions are premeditated in our mind!

Repentance reveals how deep our sin is, but also magnifies how wide God's love is for us. Gratitude from our hearts is a constant companion of repentance when we realize just how great our need for forgiveness and how merciful the God who grants it.

If it will help, list several areas of your life where you need to make repentance. Once you've done that, pray over the list and lay these things at the cross of Jesus. Ask Him to not only help you in the change of your mind, but in the change of your decisions and behaviors.

Like faith and being filled with the Holy Spirit, repentance becomes part of our growing process. We are a continual work in progress, using repentance as a vehicle to stay close to God.

Day 45
HEAVEN

We cannot even begin to fathom what heaven is like! But we know that the only way we get there when we die is our trust in Jesus Christ. Have you ever wondered if there even is a heaven and if so, what it's like?

In 2011, my husband and I were attending a lecture at the city museum. A friend of ours, a medical doctor, was lecturing.

She had ended her presentation and was allowing questions when I suddenly felt a stabbing, pain behind my right knee. I was just leaning over to tell my husband I didn't feel well when I went down. He says my head was leaning on the back of my chair and my eyes were wide open. He hollered for help and they laid me in the aisle where our doctor friend tried to tend to me.

Ten minutes or so later, I came to with paramedics hovering all around me and our doctor friend taking my pulse. She said it finally started again at 10 then gradually went up to 50 when I came to.

As we began putting all of the facts into place, apparently, I had a blood clot behind my right knee and it dislodged and went to my heart. For at least ten minutes I wasn't breathing and they couldn't find a pulse, even with CPR and pounding on my chest. Since then, they have a defib in the auditorium.

I was taken by ambulance to the hospital, which was just around the corner and as I was lying on the gurney in the hall, waiting to get a room, Paul came running down the hall to be with me. He looked like HE needed a doctor's attention! It was quite a scare

It was then that I could finally tell someone what I had experienced. I am confident that I was in heaven for those minutes.

I did not hover over my body like some have reported happening to them. I didn't see a bright light. I simply was transported to a place that is almost impossible to describe it was so beautiful and peaceful. I found myself sitting on a U-shaped split field stone bench surrounded by about a dozen people. I cannot now remember who they were, but I knew them. They were all wearing gem-stone colored ephod-like clothing. Bright blues, purples, scarlet, emerald green, even gold.

Somehow, I just knew that I was supposed to wait there, even though the green pasture in front of me, lined with tall trees blooming with flowers as colorful as the ephods, beckoned me to get closer to... what? The sky was SO blue and even though there was no sun, it was so bright. And warm! I felt warm from the inside out. And at peace. Filled with a joy that I've never known before.

Our conversation seemed to pick up from an earlier time, which I can't explain. We talked about my life and what God had been able to do in and through me so far. I knew I would return, but actually didn't even remember that I had a husband and kids to return to!

So, when I shared this with my husband, we were both pretty stunned.

This experience certainly changed me! For one, I'm confident that there IS eternal life and that heaven is real. Read Revelation 21 and 22 for the description of The New Heaven and New Earth.

Revelation 21:1 comforts us that "He will wipe away every tear from their eyes." We are told that there will be no more dying, mourning, or pain.

First Corinthians 2:9 says that heaven is INCOMPREHENSIBLE! "No eye has seen, nor ear heard, no mind has conceived what God has prepared for those who love Him."

Finally, Philippians 1:23 says that heaven will be BETTER BY FAR! Better than the best on earth. Think of it...the mere dust under our feet will be gold!

Of course, when thinking of heaven, the most important question to ask is "How do I get there?" The way is so simple. Jesus is the ONLY way. In John 14:6 Jesus tells us that "No one comes to the Father except through me."

Day 46

PROBLEMS ARE POSITIVE!

———❧———◆◉◆———❧———

You've heard it said that a beautiful pearl would never be created if it weren't for the irritation of the sand within the smooth lining of the oyster. In the same way, problems sometimes become our greatest blessing because they challenge our creativity and lead us into necessary adjustments.

In fact, problems, especially ones that seem to have no human solution, allow God to be God. Think of the problems that Christ encountered that allowed miracles to be performed: if it weren't for hungry people, the five thousand would not have been fed; if not for the blind, they would not have been given sight; if not for the sick, they would not have been healed.

When questioned by the disciples as to whose sin caused a certain man's blindness (John 9:2-3), Jesus responded, "Neither this man nor his parents sinned; but this happened so that the work of God might be displayed in His life."

When we acknowledge God's sovereign will, we recognize that there will be those occasions when He allows problems to come our way, so that the work of God might be displayed through His mighty hand of power, producing miraculous results. What a privilege to be allowed to see Him in action this way in our lives.

Problems can be positive: they cause needed change; they give us experience in avoiding future problems; they allow for creative exchange of ideas and bonding as a team; they allow us to grow and gain wisdom.

Can you look at a problem as a miraculous opportunity? Can you view a problem as a challenge to finding a creative solution? Can you accept problems as a vehicle for God's work to be displayed in your life? If you can, you will understand that if you never had a need, you might never see a miracle!

Day 47
PREVENTION PRINCIPLES

I hope you won't mind, but I've taken the liberty to put a modern-day spin on the 10 commandments. I'm calling them Prevention Principles because each one of them allows us to prevent problems in our lives if we are willing to adhere to them:

Principle #1: You shall prioritize your work, kid's schedules, shopping and time on the phone/computer so that you spend quality time with God. He MUST be the most important thing on your schedule!

Principle #2: You shall choose to worship God first rather than to sit and worship at the foot of the television set, surf the Web, or give your total devotion to another human being.

Principle #3: You shall use God's name only with reverence and awe.

Principle #4: Remember that God can only heal our troubled souls and weary bodies if we take time to rest in Him.

Principle #5: You shall show respect and meet your duty of obligation to those who have sacrificed for you and invested in your future.

Principle #6: You shall control your anger so that it does not lead to hurtful words or damaging actions.

Principle #7: Faithfulness protects us from suffering undue emotional and physical stress.

Principle #8: You shall give credit to others for even their ideas and not steal any of their recognition.

Principle #9: You shall use words and ideas that serve only to edify and build others up.

Principle $10: You will rejoice when your neighbor moves into a larger home than yours, goes on vacation, and gets a new car!

God gave us his 10 commandments not to punish us or take away our fun, but to protect us and provide for us. If we implement these prevention principles into our lives, we will reap the rewards of fewer problems, less heartache, earned respect, and God's favor.

Day 48

Outside the Camp

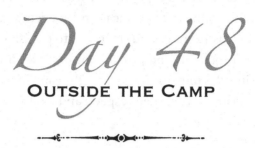

Hebrews 13:13: "Let us, then, go to him outside the camp..."

Have you ever felt that you were in a place so alone, deserted, and friendless, that it seemed as if you were at the end of the end? If so, rejoice! You are finally at a place where you will know God! God initiates incredible things "outside the camp."

In the Old Testament, God asked Moses to first erect a Tent, then build a Tabernacle "outside the camp" where they could meet. This became a place where they could meet alone and talk face to face as one man talks to another. It was here that God implemented his plan of action to guide, direct, provide order to and develop a system of worship to the Children of Israel.

In the New Testament, we find that Jesus also ended up "outside the camp" when he walked that road to Golgotha and was crucified. And on that cross, he bore alone all the sins of the world. Jesus willingly allowed himself to be led "outside the camp" so that he could deliver us from the bondage of sin. In fact, his camp was so "outside" that he was even separated from His Father as He became sin—our sin—and bore it on our behalf.

Ironically, Golgotha means "The Skull." I say that it is ironic, because when we sincerely seek more of God, we must allow even the thoughts in our head, our skull, to be crucified with Christ on that cross.

There are many things that we must put to death if we want to meet with God outside the camp; many things must be crucified if we hope to experience deliverance. When we are totally surrendered, it is then Christ who lives in and through us.

In Galatians 2:20 Paul proclaims: "I have been crucified with Christ and I no longer live, but Christ lives in me."

Day 49

NO MORE, NO LESS

In Exodus 30:11-16, God gives instruction to Moses for the offering of the "atonement for souls." God commanded that a census be taken, and everyone 20 years of age or older was to give a 1/2 shekel for this offering. One phrase that really caught my attention was this in verse 15: "The rich are not to give more than half shekel and the poor are not to give less...." In other words, the payment for atonement was the same for everyone, regardless of their financial status, blood lines, or abilities.

We've somehow become deceived within our political, educational, and yes, church systems, that there is a difference between rich and poor. I taught for a short time at a private school and was appalled when a Mom and Dad were furious at the grade their child had earned in my class. Tuition was rather expensive. Their exact words to me were, "We paid for an 'A,' now give him an A.'"

Unfortunately, this attitude permeates the church as well. Sadly, there are many examples of churches bending to certain decisions not consistent with their doctrine (or decorating sense!) who give in to the whims of those who can withhold their donation if they don't get their way.

This is contrary to the way God does things. Acts 10: 34 reminds us that "...God does not show favoritism, but accepts men from every nation who fear him and do what is right." In other offerings, men were required to give according to their ability; but for the atonement of the soul, God demands the same of each of us. There is only ONE way to the Father and that, through the blood of Jesus Christ. It is available for the very same price to each of us...And it is Jesus who paid it!

Day 50
NEAR AND FAR

Isaiah 55:6: "Seek the Lord while he may be found; call on him while he is near."

Many of us either grew up watching Sesame Street, or enjoying it with our kids. Remember Elmo? He was the character that would come so close to the camera that he was out of focus and he would state: "near." Then, we'd hear his little footsteps tap the pavement as he would hurriedly run to the backdrop and yell, "Far." Of course, he was demonstrating the relationship of proximity.

When it comes to our relationship with God, we need to live in the tension of the "near" and "far." God is BOTH "near" and "far." Aren't there times when he is so near to us that we feel his presence? Times when his grace and peace are so apparent that we know without a shadow of a doubt that he is real, loving, and very close.

Then, there are those other times when God seems "far." We've asked, but he is silent. We seek, but he is not to be found. Well, I can't explain it because we can never reach the end of who God is. As he reveals more to us about himself, we realize just how much more we don't know and understand about him. God is an infinite mystery that our finite minds will never comprehend. The more we learn of God, the more vast we see He is.

However, during those times when he does seem "far," remember the sun, the sky, and the clouds. On those days when the clouds roll in, we look up to the sky and only see the clouds. Does this mean that the sun vanished somewhere? No! Even though we cannot see the sun or feel its warmth, it is still there. And so it is with God. He is both "near" and "far."

Day 51

MOST UNWANTED

Corinthians 1:27: "But God chose the foolish...the weak...the lowly... and the despised..."

There are days when I feel unfit for service to the Lord. I mean, I just couldn't bite my tongue and had to say it; I didn't think about divorcing my husband, but perhaps could justify murder (okay, just kidding...really...just trying to be funny, but Ruth Bell Graham was once heard saying this about Billy....); my thoughts wandered from the sermon as I noticed, and coveted, several new outfits worn by fellow church members. My Salvation Army suits were starting to look frumpy. What IS God going to do with me!

I guess I'm in good company. Someone once developed a personality profile of each of the disciples and revealed that if a corporation were to be looking at their resumes as likely candidates for hire, the only one who would have made the call back pile would have been Judas!

Apparently the reason God keeps choosing me for assignments is that I closely parallel the profile laid out in I Corinthians 1:27-29: "God chose the foolish things of the world to shame the wise; God chose the weak things of the world to shame the strong. He chose the lowly things of this world and the despised things—and the things that are not—to nullify the things that are so that no one may boast before him."

You see, when we think that we can serve God from OUR wisdom, OUR strength, or OUR position, we end up thinking that we're somehow EARNING our own way to salvation. God demonstrates to us that no matter how weak, lowly, or despised we are, our salvation is totally a result of what **Jesus Christ** has done for us.

This is why the verse ends by saying, "so that no one may boast before him." When we are weak, he is strong; when we are lowly, he is lifted up; when we lack wisdom, his light shines to light our way.

Day 52

MISSION IMPOSSIBLE?

Leviticus 11:44: "I am the Lord your God; consecrate yourselves and be holy, because I am holy."

The impossible task: a square peg fitting into a round hole... walking 10 miles in two minutes....living a holy life....

Now, wait a minute! Is living a holy life REALLY an impossible task?

First of all, the Bible not only ASKS us to be holy, it COMMANDS us to be. In Leviticus 11:44 God admonishes us: "Be holy because I am Holy." Would God ask us to do something that is impossible? Of course not! However, he often asks us to do things that are difficult and that require complete dependence upon him. Such is the way of holiness.

When we come into a relationship with God, we immediately receive a degree of holiness because we are "set apart" for his service. We are stamped with his seal of ownership. We are uniquely separated TO Him. In fact, "to be holy as He is holy is based upon *His* ability to place His holiness in us through guidance, correction and grace. In this, we learn to guide, love and forgive" (Rev. Gerald Vaughn Drummonds II).

Our journey of holiness involves continuing to move closer to God the Father and farther away from our sinful nature. It involves recognizing that we will never be able to attain sin-less-ness while on this earth, and that is why we have need of the Savior Jesus Christ. His death on the cross has been accepted by God as a substitution for our death sentence. Through Jesus we are deemed holy and acceptable by God.

So, Jesus has done his part, now it's time to do ours. Holiness is simple: it means obeying the things God has asked us to do. And you know what? Adhering to his wishes protects us. When I'm faithful to my husband, I don't introduce life-threatening diseases into our home. When I'm honest in my dealings with others, I enjoy a clear conscience and am honored by God. When I strive for holiness, I rejoice that someday I will see Him face to face.

Day 53

MIRACLES

Many times throughout Scripture, we see a correlation between the size of a person's faith and the result of that faith in a miracle. When Jesus healed a woman who had been bleeding for 12 years (Matthew 9:20-22), he praises her by saying, "Daughter, your faith has healed you." When a Roman Centurion came to Jesus asking Him to heal his servant (Luke 7:1-9), Jesus exclaimed to his followers, "I tell you the truth, I have not found anyone in Israel with such great faith." When two blind men follow Jesus into the house where he was staying, he asks, "Do you believe that I am able to do this?" They respond that they do, so Jesus says, "According to your faith will it be done to you" (Matthew 9:27-30).

Does this, then, imply that if we don't see miracles or answers to our prayers that we do not have enough faith? The answer may be yes AND no!

Perhaps the more correct question to ask is: Am I giving too much attention to me and what I want and the amount of faith I want to appear to possess as opposed to putting my focus and faith totally in Jesus? Our faith must be in Christ and in Him alone. And what does it mean if we don't get the miracle we've prayed for? Most likely it means that God has a different plan—one that will allow us to see more fully His glory.

Paul was a man with great faith, yet when he prayed with faith to have God remove from him what he termed "a thorn in the flesh," God would not perform the miracle. Why? God told him, "My grace is sufficient for you, for my power is made perfect in weakness" (II Corinthians 12:9). And that is the true miracle.

Day 54

MARY

As a woman, there are times when I like to study about women who are mentioned in the Bible. I do it in hopes of trying to discover something extraordinary about them or something I can emulate to become a stronger Christian.

Probably one of the most famous women mentioned in the Bible is Mary, the mother of Jesus. Yet, there is little revealed about her. Unlike the outspoken Sarah, courageous Rahab, or faithful Ruth, a clear picture of her is never painted.

Unlike Queen Esther who had public appeal, title and wealth, Mary was a peasant girl, starting out a marriage relationship with a shroud of controversy surrounding her and probably a very small dowry.

However, Mary's life exemplifies what every person should strive for. First, no matter what her circumstances—pregnancy outside of marriage, poverty, escape from assassins, public humiliation—Mary trusted God to take care of her. She accepts His plan for her life.

Second, Mary did what God asked her to do. When the angel announces that she will bear the Messiah, her response is: "I am the Lord's servant.... May it be to me as you have said" (Luke 1:38). When an angel comes to Joseph in a dream and tells them to take the baby Jesus and escape to Egypt, they do so (Matthew 2:13-15). When Jesus hangs on the cross before her, Mary is at his feet, proving to be faithful and obedient to him right to the end.

The Scriptures don't tell us whether Mary was a leader in her community, whether she possessed musical talent, was a good cook, or whether she was handy with the embroidery needle. But what we do know is that she trusted God to take care of her and she was obedient. She leads us today by modeling what it means to love Jesus.

Day 55

MARY'S PIERCING

How would you feel if at your baby's dedication your pastor said these words to you? "This child is destined to cause the falling and rising of many...and the thoughts of many hearts will be revealed. And a sword will pierce your own soul too" (Luke 2:34-35).

I don't know about you, but if I didn't have postpartum depression before, I sure would after a comment like that!

These are the words spoken to Mary by Simeon when Mary and Joseph brought Jesus to the Temple for circumcision. Note that these words were spoken directly to Mary as if Simeon knew that she would someday face the piercing of her soul as a single Mom.

Many times throughout her son's ministry her heart would be pierced: Luke 4 records Jesus' return to Nazareth after his Temptation. His reputation as Messiah had by this time spread throughout all of Judea, yet when he returns to his home town, so strong is the town's disbelief that they riot, drag him to the outskirts of town and actually try to kill him. How it must have embarrassed and angered Mary to face the town after he left that place.

John 19 records Jesus' agony on the cross, and who stands there with him? Mary. His side is pierced as is her soul once again.

We see in Mary's piercing, however, evidence of God's great faithfulness. After Jesus' resurrection, the town and those in Jesus' family finally believe and they became the foundational support for the first church. Mary was with the disciples "joined together constantly in prayer." She would witness over 3,000 people becoming believers as Peter preached.

Yes, her soul was pierced with sorrow at times, but she was obedient to what God had called her to do. As Colossians 4:17 says, she did it "all in the name of the Lord Jesus."

Day 56

MAKING ROOM

John 14:17: "...But you know him, for he lives with you and will be in you."

Because we have moved four times in seven years, we have conducted several huge cleaning-out projects where old clothes, furniture and household items were donated. With grandchildren and lots of out of town company, there just wasn't enough room for all of these old, useless items to be stored. So, in order to make room for the new and better things, it was necessary to clean and toss out the old.

It made me think of the useless items that I treasure in my heart that need to be cleaned out. Those old resentments are taking room away from a fresh and exciting outlook. That unforgiveness is shoving away healing and joy. The pondering in my heart of past failures is squeezing room away from enjoying present successes.

God is looking to dwell in a heart that has made room for him to dwell. He cannot reside where there is jealousy, anger, hatred, or unforgiveness. God is so big that there is not room enough for him to dwell in a place where these things are strewn, rusting and rotting. He can only live in a place that has been purified and is holy...totally cleansed.

When the Children of Israel were asked by God to prepare for him a Tabernacle as his dwelling place, he left it up to them to bring the materials and build it; to prepare it willingly. If they would have refused to build it according to his specifications, then he could not dwell with them.

God has certain expectations of us that we must obey if we are to enjoy his company. It stands to reason that the more junk I remove from my heart—his dwelling place— the more of God I will get. Less of me is always more of God.

Day 57

MAGNIFY

I was sitting in choir practice, taking the next octavo out of my folder. "Magnify the Lord" was its title. Then, just like in grade school, our choir director called my name and said, "Julie, what does the word magnify mean?" My expression back to him resembled a deer caught in your headlights. Not one definition popped into my English teacher head!

I was saved, not by the bell, but by a booming voice from the bass section. In velvet tones he bellowed, "It means we should make God BIG!" We all applauded him and laughed at my uncharacteristic loss for words. Isn't that a powerful answer!

Sometimes we either make God small or don't give him credit for being as big as he is. Here's how big God is:

Hebrews 11:3 says that "the universe was formed at God's command so that what is seen was not made out of what was visible." He's our Creator. That's BIG!

In Matthew 10:29, Jesus says, "Are not two sparrows sold for a penny? Yet not one of them will fall to the ground apart from the will of our Father. He knows and ordains all earthly activity. That's BIG!

In Matthew 6:23, Jesus encourages "...do not worry about your life, what you will eat or drink, or about your body, what you will wear... look at the birds of the air; they do not sow or reap or store away in barns, and yet your heavenly father feeds them. Are you not much more valuable than they?" God provides for all our needs. That's BIG!

Matthew 9:6 tells us that "the son of man has the power to forgive sins." That's BIG!

John 3:15 assure us that "everyone who believes in Him may have eternal life." That's BIG!

Make God BIG...magnify him!

Day 58
INTERRUPTIONS

I read recently that the average office manager is interrupted at least once every six minutes. That's over 200 interruptions per day!

Frankly, nothing irritates me more than to get deeply focused on a writing assignment or project and be distracted by the phone, other conversations going on around me, or someone walking into my office uninvited!

My dear friend and Pastor, Dawn Scott Damen wrote an article called "Coming Distractions." In it she makes the observation that Jesus CAME for interruptions! She says, "He understood His mission. He was not obsessing about his own agenda but rather, He was about His Father's business." Can we say that?

She continues: "Our Savior, the Christ, was alert and on the lookout for these very strategic appointments, these human interruptions turned divine. A vacation in the mountains ends with a frantic father and a lunatic boy in need of healing, a teaching seminar comes to a screeching halt when an adulterous woman is thrown at His feet, and a sailboat ride to the islands is concluded with a demon-possessed wild man in chains serving as a tour guide. But all of these irritating disruptions found healing and forgiveness as a result of their encounter with Jesus. He did not resent them, He rescued them....He was an attraction to distraction."

I like this advice: "Place your goals in stone, but plans in sand" (Peter Zapfella). In other words, if my goal is to lead others to the Lord, that goal is solid and unchanging. However, my plans to meet that goal may take a twist and turn at times. And if it means that my current plan needs to be diverted to accommodate a divine interruption, may God give me the discernment to recognize the opportunity and embrace the interruption!

Day 59

THE WHEAT AND THE TARES

In Matthew 13, Jesus teaches about receiving and multiplying God's truth through the parable of the sower. You will recall that in this parable, the farmer scatters seed, which represents the truth of God's word. Some of the seed falls on the path where the birds eat it, some of it falls in the rocky places and takes root, but because the soil is so shallow, the roots cannot not grow deep enough to keep the plant alive. When the sun comes out, the plant withers, like those with a shallow faith.

Jesus continues the story by saying that some of the seed falls among the thorns and thistles and is choked out. Finally, the seed that falls on the good soil produces a crop that yields anywhere from 30 to 100-fold.

My word of caution today is this: Satan is a great impostor and he will try to plant what appears to be good seed into our lives. He will try to sprinkle it amongst God's seeds of truth. If we're not careful, we begin to nurture a counterfeit truth rather than God's Word.

Consider the wheat and the tare. Strangely, the tare resembles the wheat grass right up until harvest time. However, the wheat produces kernels that are nutritious and healthy, while the tare produces poisonous seeds that reproduce poisonous grass! Yikes!

Jesus makes the point that Satan often sends "pretend believers" and false doctrines into even our churches and uses them to tempt us and divert our attention from the truth of God's Word. Jesus reveals that God will let both seeds grow until his harvest. But at that time, he will "tie the weeds in bundles to be burned." However, the wheat, the harvest of our lives living in God's truth, will be brought into his barn.

Day 60

GIDEON: MIGHTY WARRIOR

Bible prophecy is so easy for us to read from our perspective, isn't it? In one sitting we can read the whole story from beginning to end and know how all the loose ends will be tied up. Living through the fulfillment of the prophecy, however, requires incredible faith.

Take, for instance, the story of Gideon. The Midianites had so ravished the Children of Israel that Judges 6 tells us they destroyed all of the crops and livestock and impoverished the Israelites. When Israel cries out to the Lord, He sends an angel to instruct Gideon.

The angel of the Lord, greets Gideon with these words: "The Lord is with you, mighty warrior" (Judges 6:12).

Now, because you and I know the end of the story, we don't think a thing about this greeting, but look at it from Gideon's perspective at this moment of time in his life. He was threshing wheat in a wine press rather than out in the open because of the enemy's threat. He was probably an upper-class aristocrat, not a soldier, and he feels incredibly inferior for he says, "My clan is the weakest...I am the least in my family" (Judges 6:15). Does this sound like a brave soldier to you? Yet the Lord acknowledges Gideon as a "mighty warrior!"

You see, God often looks at us in terms of our destiny. He looks at us in terms of his fulfilled promises and purposes for our lives. Even before we are his mighty warriors, during the times when we feel weak and that we are failures, God sees us through the eyes of our destinies—as a completed work. Philippians 1:6 confirms that "...he who began a good work in you will carry it on to completion until the day of Christ Jesus."

Day 61

EVERYDAY TASKS

I Samuel 17 documents the well-known story of David and Goliath. For 40 days this 9-foot giant of a Philistine kept taunting the Israelites. His armor weighed at least 125 pounds and it is recorded that just the handle of his sword weighed at least 15 pounds! His ranting and raving was absolutely driving the Israelite army crazy with fear.

In the meantime, a young shepherd boy, David, is asked by his father Jesse to take food up to the battle field for his three older brothers. When he sees the giant, he begins asking questions. His brothers are openly annoyed with him, but he persists to the point where he goes to King Saul and begs to have a chance at killing Goliath!

Everyone responded with disbelief. How could young David, an untrained swordsman face a foe who had been trained in warfare since childhood? And who was said to be at least NINE FEET TALL!

Here is the key point in this story. God had already prepared and equipped David for this battle through his *everyday tasks* and responsibilities. Being a shepherd required that David rescue a lamb from the jaws of a bear or lion. Many times he had used his slingshot to fall one of these great giants to protect his father's sheep.

Do you see the parallel? Often it is through *perfecting the daily tasks* we are given that God prepares us for saving his lost sheep, being his representative on the front lines, and fighting a battle.

And truly, whose battle is it? As David reminds us in I Samuel 17:47: "It is not by sword or spear that the Lord saves, for the battle is the Lords."

Day 62

DO SOMETHING!

John 9:7: "...So the man went and washed..."

Often before a miracle took place, God asked the recipient to DO something. God could have parted the Red Sea with his own hand, yet he asked Moses to "stretch your hand over the sea..." (Exodus 15:26). In fact, each of the plagues were initiated only after Aaron was obedient to lay down his staff, pick it up, or raise it.

In John 9, we read the poignant story of the blind man who received his sight. As you will recall, Jesus spat upon the ground and made a mud that he daubed upon the man's unseeing eyes. Certainly Jesus could have spoken a word and the man would have received his sight, but he asked something of him. He required that he go and wash in the Pool of Siloam. After the man did so, he came back rejoicing that his eyes could see!

The blind man represents to us things that mark the difference between actions of faith and miracles and those that produce no fruit.

Jesus tested the blind man's obedience. He performed a peculiar action, didn't he? I can't think that having someone put mud on my eyes made from their saliva would be too appealing! Then he required of this guy, who couldn't see his way, to go to a nearby pool and wash. What if the man had said to Jesus, "C'mon, give me a break! Can't you see I can't see and that this is a huge inconvenience for me to have to grope my way to this pool and wash off this disgusting mess you've placed on my eyes?"

No, he obediently followed the instructions and was made whole as a result.

Is God asking something of you and me today? Is it possible that we are just an action away from seeing a miracle?

Day 63

DON'T SETTLE

Perhaps like me, you have inadvertently shortchanged yourself when, had you just waited on God, he had something so much better planned for you.

My husband's organization moved us for a short time to a sister city that had a satellite campus. Even though we felt it would be a short stint, we decided to purchase a home in the area in hopes of turning a profit when we would eventually pack up and move "home."

In my true writer's and event planner "deadline" mind, we knew his start date and since we wanted to vacate our home in time for our son and his wife to move into it right after their wedding, I felt the pressure to get something lined up for us by a certain date.

I found the "perfect" place. Well, it did have some shortcomings. I really didn't like the corner lot. I'm a tub soaker and the master bath didn't have a tub. It had hard wood floors in places I preferred carpet. It WAS a bit pricey....but it was available and in the location we loved.

We put in the offer and were behind two other signed contracts offering more. I was in the tank! MY whole plan was off! Boo-hoo, what were we going to do? The whole world might well just stop. Oh brother. Get a grip, Jules.

We drove by the house one more time for me to lament our bad "luck," and, hey, look! There's a house for sale a few houses away, located on a huge commons. Needs some TLC, but...empty, twice the square footage, and look at the reduced price! WOW! We put in a low offer, which was accepted, and spent four glorious years living in this beautiful home with the most fabulous neighbors! And guess what? The timing could not have been more perfect.

How many times, if we are willing to wait on God and trust him, will he **SAY *NO* TO SOMETHING GOOD TO SAY *YES* TO THE BEST?**

Day 64

TIME TO SAY, "NO"

Job 37:14: "...stop and consider God's wonders."

Matthew 14:21-23 describes a rather busy and stressful day for Jesus: "The number of those who ate was about 5,000 men, beside women and children. Immediately Jesus made the disciples get into the boat and go on ahead of him...while he dismissed the crowd. After he had dismissed them, he went up on a mountainside by himself to pray."

Can you just imagine miraculously feeding with well over 10,000-15,000 people who were pressing in to ask questions, be healed, and just see you up close? And this on a dusty mountainside with no air conditioning, food vendors or porta potties! In fact, you may recall that it was during this day that Jesus fed all of them from the five loaves and two fishes. And this, after hearing about the beheading of his cousin and friend, John the Baptist. Talk about stress!

At a particular point, Jesus sees the exhaustion of his own disciples and sends them off into the water in a boat. The Word says that "he dismissed them."

This sounds to me like Jesus knew when to say "no." Certainly there were still those in the crowd who had not seen Jesus up close yet or been healed, those demanding his time, attention, and services. However, Jesus knew when he was being depleted and withdrew both his disciples and himself from the crowd so that they could be rejuvenated and refreshed.

It's often difficult for us to give ourselves permission to say "no," isn't it? However, if we don't, we serve no good purpose to anyone! Just as our car cannot run without gas, we cannot function without refueling. Saying "no" and getting some rest is one way we can be strengthened. Gather wisdom from Jesus and realize that sometimes it's okay to say "no."

Day 65

RECOVERING PERFECTIONIST

I have a friend who claims that she is a recovering...perfectionist. I'll bet that term describes many of us who desire the house to be spotless, the yard immaculate, all the laundry done, the work in the brief case completed—perfectly, of course, perfect attendance at church and school activities, and the parent of the smartest, well, all right, most perfect kids on the block.

Obviously, we can't possibly be this perfect!

Philosopher William James once said, "The art of being wise is the art of knowing what to overlook." Another philosopher promotes the idea of "planned neglect." As we all know, we can't do EVERYTHING, especially, perfectly, therefore we must choose what to overlook and neglect and what priorities to focus on. This will keep us from becoming over-committed, overwhelmed, and overbearing!

When our daughter was working full-time and taking an overload of college classes, she quickly realized that her perfectionistic tendencies would drive her insane if she did not claim and live by priorities. She chose frozen microwavable entrees over home cooked meals; she learned to reuse bath towels and send things to the dry cleaners to save time on laundry. She had to be satisfied with an occasional, quick once-over cleaning of her apartment until time permitted a more thorough job. She had to say "no" more often to social invitations.

Recovering perfectionists also have a hard time delegating. My favorite retort to this is the "Jethro Principle" found in Exodus 18. Moses' father-in-law watched as the people ran Moses dry with their issues. So, he suggested that Moses train leaders to be responsible for solving problems over thousands, hundreds, fifties, and tens.

We can conserve our precious time for eternal priorities when we learn to know what to overlook, practice planned neglect, and choose to delegate.

Day 66

MAKING THE MOST OF YOUR TIME

Are you making the most of your time? Did you know that each day we are given a gift, a deposit, in our time account of 86,400 seconds? Seneca the Younger wrote, "We are always complaining that our days are few, and acting as if there would be no end to them. Let's make haste to live since every day to a wise man it is a new life."

What are you doing with the new life that is given to you each morning? Psalms 31:15 reminds us that "My times are in your hands." We can think that we are managing our time wisely, but if our activity is not centered around the Lord's will for us, the spending of our precious 86,400 daily seconds is in vain.

James 4:13-15 explains: "Now listen, you who say, 'Today or tomorrow we will go to this or that city, spend a year there, carry on business and make money.' Why you do not even know what will happen tomorrow. What is your life? You are mist that appears for a little while and then vanishes. Instead, you ought to say, 'If it is the Lord's will, we will live and do this or that.'"

Keep in mind these issues as you decide how to spend that daily deposit of 86,400 seconds:

Does your activity and attitude glorify God?

Does your activity accomplish God's will and His goals for your life?

Does your activity accentuate eternal rather than temporal values?

Have you prayed about and submitted the spending of your time today to Him?

We can be involved in a whirlwind of activity, but if we are not accomplishing God's goals, our investment will return void. We have only the present time to spend. Perhaps there is a reason that we call today the present. It truly is a gift from God.

Day 67

KEEP YOUR COOL

Mark 4:39: "He got up, rebuked the wind and said to the waves, 'Quiet! Be still!' Then the wind died down and it was completely calm."

There are some incredibly destructive consequences that result from stress: headaches, high blood pressure, anxiety attacks, heart disease, and stroke, to name a few. 'Not a pretty picture!

Did you know that the phrases "fear not," and "don't be afraid," are said almost 500 times throughout the Bible? The word anxious or anxiety is also excessive. It's so hard for us to be calm in the middle of great stress!

Somehow Jesus was able to keep his cool in the midst of the storm—literally! Mark describes for us in chapter 4, a situation where Jesus and the disciples were crossing over the Sea of Galilee when a squall suddenly brewed up over the basin. The account reveals that it was so bad that the disciples feared being washed overboard and the boat sinking.

So, in the middle of all of this, where was Jesus? SLEEPING!

I don't know about you, but when I'm anxious, the last thing I can do is sleep. I find myself tossing and turning in the middle of the night, trying to solve the problem through my brilliant deductions and strategies, only to find that I'm even more exhausted when the sun finally rises.

Our challenge, then, is to somehow let go of our worries so that we, like Jesus, can remain calm during the turbulence of the crisis. Jesus rebuked his disciples by saying, "Why are you so afraid....Do you STILL have no faith?" Hmm...faith. Jesus expected them to have faith since he had proven himself faithful to them before.

The practice of faith can be built upon God's past faithfulness. He has a good record, you know. When we remember how God has been faithful to calm the storms of our past, we are assured that he will be there for us again.

Day 68

DELIVERANCE

Psalm 3:8: "From the Lord comes deliverance."

One of the points I make when I teach Stress Management is that dealing with stress successfully often requires us to change. And we HATE change! Change takes us out of our comfort zone and from what is familiar. But the truth is, sometimes it is IN and THROUGH change that our lives become enhanced and we fulfill our destiny.

Exodus 1:1 demonstrates this point when it reveals the dramatic changes the Children of Israel would face because "Joseph died." With his death, all the comforts and security that generation had known vanished and they were soon to be in bondage to the Egyptians. Interestingly, there was a window of time when the Children of Israel could have fled from the Egyptians in freedom, but they were too comfortable and too complacent to invite change. However, God already had a plan for their deliverance.

I want to define deliverance as not deliverance FROM, but deliverance TO their destiny. When we mail a letter, it is on the way, but until the recipient has received it, it has not been delivered.

As the story unfolds, we see that what was once God's provision for the Children of Israel becomes their prison. They are enslaved, mistreated, and abused by the Egyptians. Aha! Just as the mother Eagle places sticks in an upright position so the Eaglets cannot rest in the nest anymore, God had to make them uncomfortable so they could face change and fulfill their destiny.

Every level of adversity begins to move them in a new direction; every graduation is a new revelation. You see, often trouble sends us TO God. So the next time you are forced to change from your comfort zone, realize that often the wilderness leads to self-discovery and dependence upon God that will ultimately lead to your deliverance.

Day 69

DELEGATE THE STRESS

Exodus 18:18: "The work is too heavy for you; you cannot handle it alone."

Are you an over-achiever/perfectionist? If so, welcome to the club! My mom and dad taught me to be so picky about details. I mean, even all the soup cans (closed behind a cupboard door) had to have the labels facing outward. The towels were to be folded a particular way. Homework and piano practice had to be done before getting to go out and play. I still hold on to maintaining a high standard for the way I "perform" in every area of my life!

The problem with being a perfectionist is that we feel that we are the only ones that can do the job and do it right, therefore we end up trying to do everything all by ourselves—perfectly, of course!

Jesus knew the art of delegation. Why else would he have called 12 disciples to assist him? Granted, they were a motley crew that often performed the tasks with imperfection, but still, Jesus knew the value of delegating.

Delegating is an opportunity to mentor those who are placed within our charge—our children, our employees, our students. They can become proficient with hands-on practice.

Delegating lightens our burden. Not to use a sad example here, but it is impossible for one person—no matter how strong—to carry a casket from the hearse to the grave site. But, with six pall bearers, three on each side, the burden of placing that casket in the grave is not difficult at all.

In Exodus 17:8 we read about a battle between the Amalekites and the Children of Israel. As long as Moses held up his hands, the Israelites were winning, but when they grew too tired and he had to drop them, they began to lose. Then, "Aaron and Hur held his hands up—one on one side, one on the other..." to help them win the battle.

There are times when we, too, need to allow others to come on "one side and the other" so that we are not shouldering all the stress and responsibilities alone.

Day 70

THE CROSS REMAINS

During a trip to France a few years ago, I was amazed to look at the photos they showed us at the museum in Normandy of cities before and after the bombing of World War II. As the presenter flashed up a photo of a city before, then after the bombing, there was always one thing that remained standing, untouched by the destruction...the church building. One city's church was destroyed, but the steeple still stood tall. What a message that God was still present in the midst of tragedy!

This same truth came home to me again as I caught a portion of a recent news cast showing a church congregation moving into their new facility. Wondering where the church was located and why they had moved, I turned up the volume and moved closer to the TV.

At first what I was looking at seemed really weird to me. Many times when a church moves, the entire congregation picks up an object from the old church and in a parade walks it to the new location. That wasn't what was happening in this broadcast. Lovingly, men were tenderly holding and walking a charred cross about 10 feet tall into the new facility.

Similar to the way God reminded his people of his presence during World War II, this entire church had burned to the ground with only ashes representing its roof, walls, and furnishings. However, in the middle of the smoldering ruin, one precious item remained....the charred cross that had adorned the alcove above the pulpit.

This only remnant from their previous location serves as a reminder that no matter what our circumstances, God is faithful. No matter what calamity, God is present. No matter what is destroyed around us, the cross remains!

Day 71

STANDING STONES

--- ❦ --- ❦ ··◦··▶◀··◦·· ❦ --- ❦ ---

Joshua 4:20: "And Joshua set up at Gilgal the twelve stones they had taken out of the Jordan."

In Old Testament times there obviously were no video cameras, Youtube, or The Cloud to save and record the accounts of God's miracles! So, it was an incredible challenge for these generations to somehow create a permanent record of God's miracles so that the impact of God upon their lives would be remembered and retold.

In the book of Joshua, we discover that seven times throughout his life, Joshua commanded that a number of standing stones be erected to commemorate something of spiritual significance. The hope was that as children from the following generations would pass by, they would ask about the standing stones and what they represented. This way the stories of God's faithfulness would be preserved and passed down from generation to generation.

I believe that even today, God would be pleased if in our family circles, we would create types of "standing stones" that would remind us of and give us an opportunity to retell stories of God's faithfulness and miracles in our lives.

We've made a practice of having a sketch created that resembles the outside of the home our closest friends live in. At the bottom we have the words from Joshua 24:15 inscribed, "As for me and my house, we will serve the Lord." We date it with the date they moved in and give it as a house-warming gift. This becomes a type of "standing stone" that continually reminds that family of God's faithfulness and provision, even after they move out of that home.

Can you think of a fitting "standing stone" tradition that you can begin that will openly remind your family and friends of God's miracles and faithfulness in your life? It could be a photo album, a prayer journal, a scrapbook, or a literal standing monument. Try it today and see if this "standing stone" tradition doesn't evoke some very interesting sharing from one generation to the next!

Day 72

POURED OUT

In I Chronicles 11, we catch up with David who is being sought by Saul and about 2,000 of his soldiers. They literally want his head.

David decides to hide at the cave of Adulam which was a stronghold. Three hundred men join him there. Now, at first glance, that seems to be a good thing. They are even called "God's Mighty Men." If we go over to First Samuel's account in chapter 19, however, these "mighty men" are described as those who were in distress, in debt, or discontented. Oh, great! David's running for his life and God surrounds him with a bunch of grumpy guys trying to escape a worse reality!

We learn that the enemy army has taken Bethlehem, David's hometown. Thinking of this and perhaps the way his life was so uncomplicated as a shepherd boy there, David makes the comment that he would love a drink of water from the gate of Bethlehem.

The cave of Abdulam was 12 miles of a treacherous hike from Bethlehem, not to mention an enemy army between. However, three of his chiefs go get water from the well and bring it to David.

Then, David does the most unbelievably rude thing. He pours the water on the ground! What a waste! Or was it? Actually, David's act paralleled what they all practiced in the sacrifice of the first fruits. The spiritual correlation is that what we have comes from God and our sacrifice of giving back a portion of what he gives is an act of worship.

How often have we poured ourselves into a project or relationship just to feel that our time and treasures have been wasted? David teaches that our sacrifice makes it a sacred act of worship if it is done unto God.

Day 73

MOMENT OF VISITATION

Would you be able to recognize a "moment of visitation?"

In John 20:14, Mary almost missed it as she wept at the scene of the empty tomb: Scripture tells us that "...she turned around and saw Jesus standing there, but she did not realize that it was Jesus."

There are others in Scripture who failed to recognize their moment of visitation. After Christ's resurrection, two of his disciples were discussing all of these incredible events, including the empty tomb. As they travel on the road to Emmaus, about seven miles outside of Jerusalem, Luke 24:15: tells us that as they "discussed these things with each other, Jesus himself came up and walked along with them, but they were kept from recognizing him."

In Genesis 18, three visitors approach Abraham. As the story unfolds, it is obvious that he recognizes that two are angels and the other is the Lord himself. He recognized his moment of visitation.

When the two angels leave and go to Lot in Sodom, he also recognizes the moment of visitation. However, the towns people, men who want to have access to these two new visitors, do not recognize them as divinely appointed to meet them at that moment.

What keeps us from recognizing our moments of visitation and how can we be more perceptive in realizing them? Perhaps it's a matter of expecting the moment and being prepared for it!

I'd like to suggest that, just as a sentinel on guard, we must be on alert for signs of divine visitation. Let's watch, listen, and pray. Let's expect and LOOK for our moments of visitation! By doing so, we may experience a blessing that might otherwise pass us by.

Hebrews 13:2 reminds us: "Do not forget to entertain strangers, for by so doing some people have entertained angels without knowing it."

Day 74

IN THE HEAT OF BATTLE

Second Chronicles 20 tells of a most remarkable story involving King Jehoshaphat. Jehoshaphat learns that "a vast army" was about to attack the nation of Israel.

When he hears this, he doesn't run to his military advisors, pace the floor in anxiety, or put his head in his hands sobbing. He does what we must all do first: "he inquired of the Lord" (verse 3). He then asked the people of Judah to fast and pray with him. God honors it when we unify in his presence to inquire his will.

Jehoshaphat then renders a beautiful public prayer that ends with this declaration: "We do not know what to do, but our eyes are upon you" (verse 12).

Jahaziel, a prophet, then speaks these words from the Lord: "Do not be afraid or discouraged...FOR THE BATTLE IS NOT YOURS BUT GOD'S!" (verse 15) How many times are we afraid and discouraged in the heat of the battle? We must remember Whose battle it is!

Then, God directs Jehoshaphat to lead his army in a most unconventional manner. Imagine, had they had telephones then, this conversation: "Hello, is this Zebadiah? Hi, this is Jehoshaphat...you know, king? Well, we're facing a challenging battle tomorrow and...well, don't you sing tenor? Bass is fine. Well, here's the deal....I need you to gather up a bunch of guys from the men's vocal band and go ahead of the troops and sing. No, no swords. Just your voices. Hello? Zebadiah?"

The story continues: "Jehoshaphat appointed men to sing to the Lord and praise him...as they went out ahead of the army: 'Give thanks to the Lord for his love endures forever.' As they began to sing and praise, the Lord set ambushes against the men...and they were defeated" (verse 22). And so will our enemies as we sing God's praises!

Day 75

HYSSOP

II Samuel 11-12 records the incident in King David's life when he murdered a man because he committed adultery with that man's wife. Both sins, under the law, dictated death to the perpetrator.

David is confronted about his sin by the prophet Nathan and finally, David falls to the ground truly repentant. In verse 7 David says, "Cleanse me with hyssop and I will be clean; wash me, and I will be whiter than snow." When we sin, we feel dirty and stained. We long to be purified and cleansed. There is a symbolic significance to the reference of the hyssop plant. It points back to Jewish law, and foreshadows Jesus' death on the cross.

The hyssop is a plant that is a part of the marjoram family. It grows to be about three feet tall, produces a yellow flower, and spreads freely in rocky crevices. In Jewish history, the hyssop is significant because it was used in purification ceremonies and was dipped in blood, then sprinkled upon the door posts at the first Passover.

If we fast-forward to the New Testament, John 19:28-30 describes Jesus' last moments on the cross. It's interesting to note that Jesus had refused to drink a concoction of wine and gall (or myrrh) which often numbed pain, but He accepted wine vinegar and hyssop. It was hyssop that ushered in the first Passover and hyssop that was in the last cup Jesus would drink—as He spilled His blood, covering our sins once and for all.

This hyssop or marjoram spice can still today serve as a reminder to us of Jesus' cleansing power over sin. I would encourage you to add it to soup and meat recipes and as you do, bow your head with me and repent of any sins committed against God.

Day 76

HUMANITY MEETS DIVINITY

Isaiah 41:19: "I will put in the desert the cedar and the acacia..."

Sometimes I'm still amazed at the way God surfaces an idea in the Old Testament as a foreshadowing of its fulfillment in the New Testament. One such symbolic element can be found beginning in Exodus 25:23 as God is instructing Moses on how to construct the furniture in the Holy of Holies.

"Make a table of acacia wood...and overlay it with pure gold..." are the first instructions. What is so interesting about this is that the Holy of Holies represents the place where humanity meets divinity. Scholars point out that this is the first time the term "table" is used in the Bible. It is a prophecy of Psalms 23:5 where David says: "You prepare a table before me in the presence of my enemies." In the choosing of the materials for the construction of the table, God continues to symbolize and confirm that he wants to meet with us.

They tell us that acacia wood is an incorruptible wood that even insects cannot not fester within and ruin. It probably is tough because it is a product of the wilderness. Already we can see that the wood represents the Children of Israel who wondered in the wilderness.

Next, God tells them to overlay the acacia wood with pure gold. Often, gold is used to represent purity or divinity. Isn't this a beautiful picture of God covering and protecting his people through his strength and purity!

Finally, and most importantly, when we apply the symbolism of the wood and the purity of the gold covering it, isn't it a beautiful illustration of what Christ did for us on the cross? There, sinless, blameless, and pure, Divinity was wrapped around a cross made of wood; wood that represents our humanity. The cross is the place where divinity reached down to forever change humanity.

Day 77

IN EVERY LINE

Hebrews 4:12: "For the word of God is living and active."

One year at the Christian Booksellers conference, a fellow author named Lee Ezell came up to me with a big smirk on her face and handed me a book she had written. Her sparkle radiated that this was one of her proudest achievements.

Anxious to "ooh and ah" over this great accomplishment I eagerly searched out the title. The cover design reminded me a lot of the famous "Men are from Mars, Women are from Venus" book. There were genetic symbols for the genders and the title: "What Men Understand About Women."

Hmm....pretty thick book for that, I thought. Quickly, I thumbed to the table of contents wanting to skim the chapter titles. Not finding it, I flipped over a few more pages. Nothing. I fanned the entire book. Every page was blank!

Aren't you thankful that as we open the Word of God the pages are FILLED with information to help us understand Who GOD is? Each story reveals revelations about his character and His love.

One of my favorite scripture passages that totally defines God is where God himself describes himself to Moses. Exodus 34:6 begins "And he (God) passed in front of Moses, proclaiming, 'The Lord the Lord, the compassionate and gracious God, slow to anger, abounding in love and faithfulness, maintaining love to thousands, and forgiving wickedness, rebellion and sin.'"

From this point on, in every line of Scripture, God's acts of justice, mercy, and love underscore each of these character traits. Of course,

His most precious act of compassion, faithfulness, forgiveness and love, hung on a cross in our place so that we might forever experience God. God's ways are revealed in His Word. He can be found in every line.

Day 78

COME TO THE TABLE

Revelation 19:9: "...Blessed are those who are invited to the wedding supper of the Lamb."

When I was growing up, one of the highlights of a day was skipping in the back door and asking my Mom what was for dinner. When meal time rolled around, it was fun to catch up with each other's day and my Dad always had a good joke or pun for the day.

Where has the dinner hour disappeared to these days? It's being gobbled up in soccer practice, tennis matches, rehearsals, late meetings, and many other worthwhile functions. But it is sad that most families are lucky to share even two meals together in a week.

The idea of sitting around a table for fellowship was God's idea. He initiated this in Exodus 25 through the instructions he gave Moses for placing the showbread on this special grain offering table. Symbolically, the priests made one big batch of unleavened dough, then divided it into twelve loaves representing each of the twelve tribes of Israel. What began as one piece is broken into many parts, much like the church. I Corinthians 10:17 says "Because there is one loaf, we, who are many, are one body, for we all partake of the one loaf."

God also instructed that a rim be constructed around the edge of the table so that not even the crumbs would drop from it to the floor. Our Father does not want any of us to be lost. In verse 30, He calls this the "bread of Presence." He wants to commune with us and when we come to His table, he is always there to meet us—He is ever-present. Luke 22: 19: "And he took the bread, gave thanks and broke it, and gave it to them, saying, "This is my body given for you; do this in remembrance of me." From Jesus, the Bread of Life, we receive nourishment and restoration.

Day 79

THOU SHALT NOT STEAL

Ephesians 4:28: "He who has been stealing must steal no longer..."

One day I reluctantly agreed to meet with a woman I had never met who wanted to "get to know me." Since she was visiting from another city, I caved in and squeezed in a breakfast meeting on my way to the airport.

At the agreed time and place, I arrived. After 15 minutes of waiting in the lobby, I walked around the restaurant, seeing no woman waiting, and then down to the connecting hotel to see if perhaps I had made a mistake and she was waiting there. She was not, so I paced another 15 minutes and finally called her room in the hotel. No answer. Finally, I ate a quick breakfast and headed off to the airport.

All I could think of was, "how rude!" She took something from me that is very precious because it is at a premium: my time.

Now, this woman would probably never stick her hand into my purse and lift a 10-dollar bill, but in the very same sense, she had stolen something from me that was valuable and irreplaceable.

This isn't the only thing that we steal from others. Have you ever worked so hard on a project only to have someone else take all the credit! Again, this person would never consider taking an item off your desk or stealing your purse or wallet, but by taking credit for your accomplishment, this person has surely stolen from you!

As Jesus tells us in Luke 6:31: "Do to others as you would have them do to you." When we rob someone of their precious time, or do not allow them to receive the credit they are due, just as if we took a valuable vase from their China cabinet, we have stolen! Let's remember this the next time we are tempted take another's time or receive undeserved credit.

Day 80

THE EGG, THE CARROT, AND THE COFFEE BEAN

When you face trials and adversity, do you respond like a carrot, an egg, or coffee beans?

One day when a very discouraged young lady began complaining to her father at how hard life had been, he, a professional chef, led her into the kitchen. He proceeded to fill three sauce pans on burners with water and turned the temperatures on high. He placed carrots in one sauce pan, eggs in the next, and ground coffee beans in the third.

He allowed each pot to boil for a half hour. He then removed the carrots and eggs and strained the coffee into a mug.

Turning to his daughter he said, "So, what do you see?" She rolled her eyes and said, "Duh, carrots, eggs, and coffee." "Yes, but feel the carrots now. Touch the eggs. Sip the coffee. Now tell me what you observe."

"Well," she stumbled. "The boiling water made the carrots soft and the eggs hard. And that coffee...well it's the strongest I've ever tasted!"

"Precisely!" he beamed. "You see, if you face adversity like a carrot, the smallest amount of pain makes you wilt and become soft with no strength. If you face hard times like an egg, your shell may look the same, but inside you are bitter and tough with a hardened heart. However, if you allow trials to affect you like the coffee bean, you discover that they just make you stronger!" (heavensinspirations.com).

I don't know about you, but I want to be a coffee bean! Second Corinthians 4:8, 9, and 17 remind us that "We are hard-pressed on every side, but not crushed; perplexed, but not in despair; persecuted, but not abandoned; struck down, but not destroyed. For our light and momentary troubles are achieving for us an eternal glory that far outweighs them all."

Day 81
GOOD WORDS

Proverbs 17:4 tells us that starting a quarrel is like breaching a dam. So, the opposite must be true too—when we stop quarrelling, it's like releasing life-giving, cleansing water.

Proverbs 15:1 reminds us that "a gentle answer turns away wrath, but a harsh word stirs up anger." Verse 4 tells us that our tongue can be a tree of life, or if it is deceitful, it can crush the spirit.

Proverbs 26:20 says, "Without wood a fire goes out; without gossip a quarrel dies down." Gossip, quarrels, and harsh words have the power to break friendships.

To build and maintain friendships, the Word tells us that we need to speak new words from a new source. And that source is God's words of grace. What does the Bible tell us about God's words? Well, Proverbs 30:5 says, "every word of God's is flawless; he is a shield to those who take refuge in Him."

Like God's words, then, we must set our heart on speaking words of purity and truth. And when others try to spear us or shower us with hurtful words, God becomes our shield, protecting us from them.

When we use God's words, Proverbs 15:4 tells us we bring healing. Proverbs 25:11 says our words become like apples of gold in settings of silver. Apples represent fruit, which is symbolic of wisdom. Gold and silver are priceless.

Do you wish to hear kind words? Then, speak them!

Do you long to be protected from words that are intended to crush your spirit? Let God be your shield.

Do you hope for new relationships? Build new friendships by using words of grace from God the Father.

Day 82
ONE OF US

Mark 9:38 begins a conversation between Jesus and His disciples concerning someone who was not "one of us." I hate to say it, but I can almost hear whining in this comment from John to Jesus: "Teacher, we saw a man driving out demons in your name and we told him to stop, because he was not one of us."

Now, the unknown man is not named, but we can probably deduce something about him. We can assume that he embraced the name of Jesus and that God authenticated his ministry by allowing him to cast out demons. Even though he is not a member of the inner circle, the 12 disciples, he is able to perform supernatural works.

I have to believe that there is an inkling of jealously going on here. You see, if you go back in the Scriptures to verse 17, we find that the disciples were NOT able to cast out a demon, yet this unknown man, not a part of this fellowship, WAS able to do it!

Doesn't this remind us of the unnecessary bad feelings that sometimes evolve between different denominations? Aren't there times when we see success in someone else's ministry and try to belittle it because it wasn't born through our church affiliation… "one of us?"

The Bible helps us define who is "one of us." In I John 4:1-3, we are encouraged to "test the spirits." We know it is the true spirit of God if the person acknowledges God and the name of Jesus. This incident also teaches us that we are better off to cooperate, rather to compete with others who are doing God's work. Sometimes we spend so much energy fighting each other that we fail to unite against our common enemy, Satan.

Day 83

NOT ULTIMATE DEFEAT

There seem to be only a handful of biblical characters that did not do some pretty stupid things. Abraham just about blew it when he passed his wife Sarah off as his sister to Pharaoh. The lie led to disease among Pharaoh's house (Genesis 12:10-20).

David plotted a murder and committed adultery (Second Samuel 10-12).

Moses would not have been named poster boy for best behaved either. He not only killed a man (Genesis 2:11-15), but then ran away as a coward. When he did return to lead his people out of captivity, he continued to make blunders. Even though he spoke directly with God as if he was his friend, his disobedience prevented him from ever getting to cross over into the Promised Land (Exodus Deuteronomy 34: 4).

But wait! There's more! Jonah refused to obey God and preach the Gospel in Nineveh. He ran in exactly the opposite direction to Tarshish hoping to escape his assignment. As you recall, a great fish swallowed Jonah and three days later spit him out on the shore of...guess where? Nineveh! (Jonah 1:1-17)

Peter, who had walked with and served Jesus in his ministry for three years denied even knowing him (John 18).

Each of these men, specifically chosen by God to serve him in a very special way, had their moments of weakness and failure. By the actions of their own decisions, they experienced defeat. However, if we read the "rest of the story," we find that these momentary times of defeat did not lead to ultimate defeat.

Of Abraham, James 2:23 concludes, "Abraham believed God and it was credited to him as righteousness." Hebrews 3:5 says, "Moses was a faithful servant in God's house." David was still known as "A man after God's own heart" (I Samuel 13:14). Perhaps you and I will also suffer temporary defeats, but we must be encouraged that that does not mean ultimate defeat!

Day 84

CREATIVE CHALLENGES

When I was a student at Spring Arbor University in the mid-seventies, Dr. Woody Voller was president. Now, he was a perfect mixture of John Wayne and Ronald Reagan. His greatest asset was his optimism. My husband, who worked on staff, quickly adopted Dr. Voller's philosophy that there are no insurmountable problems, only opportunities for creative solutions.

Have you ever looked at an obstacle as something positive? Dr. Voller did. He realized that every moving object will experience resistance, but setbacks can actually propel us forward if we let them.

Alexander Graham Bell is quoted as saying, "When one door closes, another opens; but we often look so long and regretfully upon the closed door that we do not see the one which has opened for us." Obstacles often change our direction, but they do not need to deter us from our destination. We must diligently search for the open door.

Proverbs 27:17 reminds us that "As iron sharpens iron, so one man sharpens another." This implies that friction, possibly in the form of failure, disappointment, or criticism brings us to the best outcome. Obstacles can defeat us, or they can sharpen us. They can tempt us to quit, or they can propel us to continue. We have the ability to choose which outcome we will experience.

Think of the setbacks and obstacles Abraham Lincoln faced before finally being elected president. He was defeated six times for public office, lost his job, failed in business, and even suffered a nervous breakdown. Yet, each obstacle served to equip, prepare, and strengthen him for the office of president. Each crisis he faced shaped his character and provided the wisdom he would need to lead our country through division and civil war.

We must remember that a diamond cannot be polished without friction, nor the person perfected without trials.

Day 85

BIBLE ANSWERS

When we are faced with trials and setbacks, where can we go for comfort? One of the first places we can turn is to the Word of God. Consider this:

When you feel that it's impossible, remember what Jesus said in Luke 18:27: "What is impossible with men is possible with God."

When you feel you're "too tired," Jesus assures us in Matthew 11:28: "...I will give you rest."

When you're convinced that: "Nobody really loves me," John 3:16 tells us that "For God so loved the world that he gave His one and only son..."

When you feel like you just: "can't go on," we can take comfort that "My grace is sufficient" (II Corinthians 12:9).

Do you ever think that you: "can't figure things out?" Proverbs 20:24 declares that "a man's steps are directed by the Lord."

When you think: "I just can't do this," Philippians 4:13 reminds us that: "I can do everything through him who gives me strength."

You may feel that: "It's not worth it." Romans 8:28 encourages us that it will be worth it: "And we know that in all things God works for the good of those who love him, who have been called according to his purpose."

Perhaps you scream: "How can God ever forgive me!" Remember what God says in First John 1:9: "If we confess our sins, he is faithful and just to forgive us our sins..."

You may ask: "How can I manage?" Philippians 4:19 assures us that God "will meet all your needs..."

When you are afraid, Second Timothy 1:7 says: "God has not given you a spirit of fear."

Are there times when you feel all alone? Hebrews 13:5 assures us He will "never leave you."

So, where do we go when we face trials and doubts? Let's RUN to the word of God!

Day 86
GOD'S WORDS

The Bible is a miraculous compilation of history, prophecy, and insight that can encourage us through even the darkest moments. This is why it is so important for us to spend time in the Word!

If you're having trouble staying above the clouds today, let me share some passages that will bring you up a notch or two.

Second Corinthians 1:3 tells us that God is "the God of all comfort." Verse 10 tells us that "he will deliver us!" Chapter 4 verse 8 says, "We are hard pressed on every side, but not crushed; perplexed, but not in despair; persecuted, but not abandoned; struck down, but not destroyed." Chapter 7 verse 6 tells us that God "comforts the downcast."

Ephesians 2:14 reminds us that God "himself is our peace."

Philippians 1:6 says, "He who began a good work in you will carry it on to completion…."

Philippians 1:21: "For to live is Christ; to die is gain."

Philippians 4:19: "And my God will meet all your needs according to his glorious riches in Christ Jesus."

James 5:11: "The Lord is full of compassion and mercy."

John 16:24: "Ask and you will receive, and your joy will be complete."

John 10:10: "I have come that you may have life, and have it to the full."

Finally, Jesus' own words in John 14:27 encourages us that "Peace I leave with you; my peace I give you. I do not give to you as the world gives. Do not let your hearts be troubled and do not be afraid." And John 16:33: "In this world you will have trouble. But take heart! I have overcome the world."

Day 87

OIL IN MY LAMP

Psalms 61:1-3: "The Spirit...bestow(s) the oil of gladness..."

When I was a child attending Sunday School, one of the songs we would sing was, "Give me oil in my lamp, keep it burning, burning, burning. Give me oil in my lamp I pray. Give me oil in my lamp keep it burning, burning, burning, keep it burning 'til the break of day" (anonymous/traditional hymn). The song was based upon the parable of the Ten Virgins in Matthew 25, teaching us to be ready at all times for Christ's return.

In addition, it is a continuing Old Testament theme that New Testament Christians could readily understand. In the Tabernacle of Moses, the Holy of Holies contained three furnishings: a lamp stand, a table for the showbread, and the altar of Incense. The first thing that would be seen by the priests as they entered this Holy place was the lamp stand. With its seven arms aflame with fire, it represented perfection. Jesus is the light of the world, perfect and spotless.

The fire was to burn continually, so rather than using candles which consume themselves, God commanded them to use oil. The type of oil required was a precious ingredient, having been crushed, beaten and pressed clear. Jesus was bruised for our iniquities. The oil was continually replenished so that the fire would not go out.

When we become Christians, the Holy Spirit immediately indwells us as a light that flows and emanates through us. However, in order for our fire to continually burn, we need to continually be filled with the Holy Spirit. When Ephesians 5:18 reminds us that we need to "... be filled with the Spirit," the verb tense used suggests that our filling is not a once and for all experience, but that our portion needs to be continually replenished. Come, again, Holy Spirit, fill us....

Day 88
OUR REFUGE

Psalm 46:1 says, "God is our refuge and strength, an ever-present help in trouble."

Webster's Dictionary defines a refuge as "a shelter from danger; protection from distress or difficulty; a course of action providing protection." When we take refuge, we put ourselves in a place—in the hand of God, which shelters and protects.

So, if God is our refuge, he is a place where we can go for strength and help. When we do this, we enjoy the benefits described in the next verse: "Therefore we will not fear..."

There are several practical applications that result when we take refuge in God. First of all, we can relax! Verse 10 says, "Be still and know that I am God." The next part reads "I will be exalted among the nations, I will be exalted in the earth." I'm told that the actual verb tense used really says, "I AM exalted!"

Next, taking refuge allows us to refocus. When we settle our focus on God, we take it off of the other gods in our lives: finances, material goods, and self-centeredness. When we refocus, we are more aware of God's good Creation. When you finally do stop to smell some roses, don't you feel better? Look at the sunrise and the moon! Notice the changing color on the leaves and the snow. Refocus!

Then, as Psalms 62:8 remind us, "Pour out your hearts to him, for God is our refuge." Praying puts us in the safe haven of God's protection. Finally, we can take refuge in God's Word. When we are consumed by fear, we should repeat Psalms 91:1and 2: "He who dwells in the shelter of the Most High will rest in the shadow of the Almighty... He is my refuge and my fortress, my God, in whom I trust."

Day 89

DECISIONS

In Luke 5:1-11 we find Jesus by the lake of Gennersaret. Because of a great multitude of people pressing in upon Jesus, he needed to position himself so that he could be seen and heard. Close by were two empty fishing boats, abandoned by their fishermen who were washing their nets on shore.

One of the boats belonged to Simon, so Jesus asked him if he would put out a little from land so he could sit in the boat and teach from there. Simon had a decision to make...and he decided to comply with the request.

After Jesus finished speaking, he turned to Simon and made another request. "Put out into the deep water and let down the nets for a catch" (Luke 5:4).

Simon responded, "Master, we've worked hard all night and haven't caught anything. But because you say so, I will let down the nets" (Luke 5:5).

Simon had another decision to make. This request didn't make sense to him. You see, a seasoned fisherman like Simon knew that the best fishing was done at night in the shallow waters. Jesus was asking him to throw out his nets during the day into deep water.

Peter was faced with a life-changing decision. Although the facts told him one thing, he considered the Source making the request and decided to obey. He and Jesus cast off from shore together. As a result of obeying Jesus, this time when he lowered the nets, they caught so many fish that his nets began to break!

This story contains several interesting points. The first is, when we face making decisions, we must be obedient to God no matter what the facts may tell us. Second, we need to remember that just as Jesus was in the boat with Simon that day, He is always with us when we are obedient to Him. Finally, we need to remember that we might only know God's partial blessing because we stop short of obedience. God wants us to draw closer to Him—especially in the midst of making decisions.

Day 90
AMEN

Revelation 3:14 reads, "These are the words of the Amen, the faithful and true witness, the ruler of God's creation."

We often use the word Amen, don't we? Where did it come from and what does it mean? We use it as the closure to a prayer or a word we may say when the pastor really makes an inspiring remark. It confirms a statement or an oath. Technically, it means "so be it." When God said, "Let there be light," he spoke it and it was...so be it (Genesis 1:3).

Isaiah 65:16 calls the Lord "the God of truth." In the original Hebrew, this literally means, the "God of Amen." One commentator said, "This is Isaiah's way of saying that the Lord is the One who remains eternally true, the One who can always be relied on."

Nehemiah 5:13 records how the people responded to Nehemiah's exhortation to the Jewish nation to unify: "At this the whole assembly said, 'Amen,' and praised the Lord." In Nehemiah 8:6, when Ezra prepared to read the Book of Law, he opened the book and all the people stood up. "...all the people lifted their hands and responded, 'Amen! Amen!' Then they bowed down and worshiped the Lord with their faces to the ground."

As I read from Revelation 3:14, the word Amen in the New Testament becomes another name for Jesus Christ—and he, crucified, risen, and sitting at the right hand of the Father. The Amen is eternally true, he is reliable, he is faithful, he is the true witness, the ruler of God's creation. He is worthy of our praise, he is worthy for us to raise our hands to, he is worthy for us to bow down to, he is worthy for us to worship with our faces to the ground. Amen. So be it...

Printed in the United States
By Bookmasters